The little PIZZA cookbook

The little PIZZA cookbook

MURDOCH BOOKS

SYDNEY · LONDON

CONTENTS

INTRODUCTION

*Pizza began life as a fast food,
eaten hot on the backstreets of
Naples. Today it is found all over
the world, but it is still in Naples
that skilled* pizzaioli *(pizza-makers)
use wonderful local tomatoes,
mozzarella cheese and basil to produce
the finest of pizzas.*

Pizza, in the sense of a flat bread covered with toppings, has probably been around since the ancient Greeks and Romans, and many regions developed their own versions. However, it is the pizza of Naples that has come to be regarded as the true pizza. The first Neapolitan pizzas were white, made with garlic, lard, salt and anchovies. It was the tomato that was to transform pizza and the Neapolitans were the first Europeans to embrace this new fruit, growing them from seeds brought from the New World. The first tomato pizza was probably the classic marinara.

By the mid-nineteenth century, pizzerias had opened in Naples and wandering vendors sold slices to people on the streets. A way of life was born for the Neapolitans and their pizza began to achieve wider notoriety, with visitors venturing into poor neighbourhoods to sample this new food. When Queen Margherita visited in 1889, she too wanted to try the famous pizza. A *pizzaiolo* named Raffaele Esposito was summoned and he created a pizza of mozzarella cheese, tomatoes and basil based on the colours of the Italian flag—later to be named after the Queen.

Pizza is the classic fast food and today in Naples traditional round pizzas are baked to order, then folded into quarters and wrapped in paper to take away. Elsewhere, it is more usual to find *pizza a taglio*—pizza that has been baked in a large tray and sold by the slice. Probably originating in Rome, *pizza a taglio* can be ordered by weight in many places and reheated as a snack or lunch.

Associazione Vera Pizza Napoletana (The True Neapolitan Pizza Association) has been set up to safeguard the pizza. Their guidelines include that the dough must be made only from flour, yeast, salt and, water and it must not be worked by machine. Pizzas are to be cooked directly on the floor of a brick-or stone-lined wood-fired oven and the temperature must exceed 400°C (750°F /Gas 6). The *cornicione* (border) must be high and soft and the whole crust not too crisp. A pizza should take only 12 minutes to cook and should be brown and crisp with the ingredients melted together.

Emigrating Neapolitans took pizza with them to America and, by the 1950s, pizza could probably be found more easily in America than in the north of Italy. When the rest of Italy did take to pizza, they adapted it to their own tastes: the Roman pizza has more topping, is thinner and crisper, and does not have a border.

Chapter 1

TRADITIONAL

◇◇

*Traditional pizzas often include those ingredients that we instantly
associate with a great-tasting pizza—rich, chunky tomato paste,
fresh aromatic basil and thick, stringy mozzarella cheese.*

Pizza napoletana

Neapolitana pizza

The true Pizza Napoletana has just two ingredients: tomato sauce and cheese. This recipe is one of many variations and adds olives, anchovies and capers to the basic topping.

Preparation time: 10 minutes
Cooking time: 12 minutes
Makes: two 30 cm (12 in) square pizzas (serves 4–6)

1 quantity pizza dough (see page 168)
1 quantity pizza sauce (see page 169)
340 g (12 oz/2²/₃ cups) coarsely grated
  mozzarella cheese

125 g (4½ oz/1 cup) pitted black olives
60 g (2¼ oz/⅓ cup) capers, rinsed, drained
16 anchovy fillets, drained on paper towel,
  halved lengthways

Preheat the oven to 220°C (425°F/Gas 7). Place two large, heavy baking trays in the oven to heat.

Cut the dough into two even portions and shape each into a ball. Press each ball to flatten, then use a lightly floured rolling pin to roll out each ball on a piece of non-stick baking paper to a 30 cm (12 in) square. Spread the pizzas evenly with the pizza sauce, then top with the mozzarella cheese, olives, capers and anchovies.

Remove the trays from the oven one at a time to keep them as hot as possible and carefully slide one pizza (still on the baking paper) onto each tray.

Bake for 12 minutes, swapping the trays around halfway through cooking, or until the bases are crisp and golden, and the mozzarella cheese is bubbling. Serve immediately.

Prosciutto, bocconcini & rocket pizza

'Prosciutto' is Italian for ham, but the term is widely used to describe any seasoned, cured, air-dried ham. For best results use very thinly sliced proscuitto from your local delicatessan.

Preparation time: 15 minutes
Cooking time: 24 minutes
Makes: four 24 cm (9½ in) round pizzas (serves 4)

2½ tablespoons extra virgin olive oil, plus extra, for drizzling
2 garlic cloves, crushed
1 quantity pizza dough (see page 168)
440 g (15½ oz) bocconcini (fresh baby mozzarella cheese), drained on paper towel, torn into 2 cm (¾ in) chunks

150 g (5½ oz) thinly sliced prosciutto, roughly torn lengthways
50 g (1¾ oz) rocket (arugula) leaves
125 g (4½ oz/½ cup) olive tapenade (see page 172)

Preheat the oven to 220°C (425°F/Gas 7). Place two large, heavy pizza or baking trays in the oven to heat.

Combine the olive oil and garlic in a small bowl and stir to combine well.

Cut the dough into four even portions and shape each into a ball. Press each ball to flatten, then use a lightly floured rolling pin to roll out each ball on a piece of non-stick baking paper to a 24 cm (9½ in) round. Brush each pizza with some of the garlic oil.

Remove the trays from the oven one at a time to keep them as hot as possible and carefully slide one pizza (still on the baking paper) onto each tray.

Bake the pizzas for 8 minutes. Remove the pizzas from the oven and top with half the bocconcini, scattering evenly. Return the pizzas to the oven, swapping the trays around, and bake for a further 3–4 minutes or until the bocconcini starts to melt and the bases are crisp and golden. Repeat with the remaining two pizzas and bocconcini.

Serve the pizzas immediately, scattered with the prosciutto and rocket, topped with a little of the tapenade and drizzled with extra olive oil. Serve the remaining tapenade passed separately.

Margherita pizza

Red tomatoes, fresh white mozzarella cheese and green basil. The toppings of this traditional pizza—supposedly named in honour of Queen Margherita of Italy in 1889—reflect the colours of the Italian flag.

Preparation time: 10 minutes
Cooking time: 12 minutes
Makes: four 26 cm (10½ in) round pizzas (serves 4)

1 quantity pizza dough (see page 168)
185 ml (6 fl oz/¾ cup) pizza sauce (see page 169)
150 g (5½ oz) bocconcini (fresh baby mozzarella cheese), thinly sliced

olive oil, for drizzling
small basil leaves, to garnish

Preheat the oven to 230°C (450°F/Gas 8). Place two large, heavy pizza or baking trays in the oven to heat.

Cut the dough into four even portions and shape each into a ball. Press each ball to flatten, then use a lightly floured rolling pin to roll out each ball on a piece of non-stick baking paper to a 26 cm (10½ in) round.

Spread the pizzas evenly with the pizza sauce, leaving a small border. Top with the bocconcini and drizzle with a little olive oil.

Remove the trays from the oven one at a time to keep them as hot as possible and carefully slide one pizza (still on the baking paper) onto each tray. Bake for 10–12 minutes, swapping the trays around halfway through cooking, or until the bases are crisp and golden. Bake the remaining two pizzas.

Serve immediately, sprinkled with the basil.

Mushroom & herb pizza with pesto

Pizza first existed as a bread to accompany meals. The original topping for a *pizza bianca* (white pizza) was garlic, lard, salt and anchovies.

Preparation time: 20 minutes
Cooking time: 30 minutes
Makes: four 25 cm (10 in) square pizzas (serves 4)

1 tablespoon olive oil
1 large brown onion, cut into thin wedges
2 garlic cloves, sliced
2 x 400 g (14 oz) tinned whole tomatoes
1 quantity pizza dough (see page 168)
160 ml (5¼ fl oz/⅔ cup) pizza sauce
  (see page 169)
250 g (9 oz) fresh buffalo mozzarella cheese,
  thinly sliced

2 large mushrooms (about 240 g/8½ oz), trimmed,
  peeled, cut into 8 mm (³/₈ in) slices
1 small handful chopped flat-leaf (Italian) parsley
1 small handful sage
105 g (3½ oz/½ cup) pesto (see page 173)
80 ml (2½ fl oz/⅓ cup) extra virgin olive oil

Heat the olive oil in a large frying pan over medium heat. Add the onion and cook, stirring occasionally for 5–6 minutes or until softened. Add the garlic and cook for 1 minute, stirring constantly so the garlic and onion do not take on too much colour. Transfer to a plate to cool.

Meanwhile, drain the tinned tomatoes in a colander. Squeeze gently in the palm of your hand to extract most of the seeds and juice. Place on paper towel to absorb excess moisture.

Preheat the oven to 230°C (450°F/Gas 8). Place two large, heavy baking trays in the oven to heat.

Cut the dough into four even portions and shape each into a ball. Press each ball to flatten, then use a lightly floured rolling pin to roll out each ball

on a piece of non-stick baking paper to a 25 cm (10 in) square.

Spread the pizzas evenly with the pizza sauce, top with the onion mixture, half the mozzarella cheese, tomatoes, mushroom slices, parsley, sage and then the remaining mozzarella cheese.

Remove the trays from the oven one at a time to keep them as hot as possible and carefully slide one pizza (still on the baking paper) onto each tray. Bake for 10–12 minutes, swapping the trays around halfway through cooking, or until the bases are crisp and golden. Bake the remaining two pizzas. Combine the pesto and extra virgin olive oil, and drizzle over the top of the pizzas. Serve immediately.

Potato & rosemary pizza

Desiree potatoes have a creamy yellow flesh and smooth red skin. Their firm texture makes them ideal for this recipe. You could also use Pontiac, Red Rascal, Royal Blue Sebago or any other variety of potato with a firm texture.

Preparation time: 20 minutes
Cooking time: 25–30 minutes
Makes: two 30 cm (12 in) round pizzas (serves 6–8 as a starter)

1 quantity pizza dough (see page 168)
2 tablespoons olive oil
2 garlic cloves, crushed
2 potatoes (such as desiree) (about 300 g/10½ oz), unpeeled, very thinly sliced

1 tablespoon rosemary leaves, plus extra, to garnish
1 teaspoon salt

Preheat the oven to 220°C (425°F/Gas 7). Cut the dough into two even portions and shape each into a ball. Press each ball to flatten, then use a lightly floured rolling pin to roll out each ball on a piece of non-stick baking paper to a 30 cm (12 in) round. Transfer the pizzas (still on the baking paper) to two large, heavy pizza or baking trays.

Mix 2 teaspoons of the olive oil with the garlic and brush evenly over the pizzas. Gently toss the remaining olive oil, potato, rosemary, salt and freshly ground black pepper, to taste, in a bowl. Arrange the potato slices in overlapping circles over the pizzas. Drizzle with any oil remaining in the bowl.

Bake the pizzas for 25–30 minutes, swapping the trays around halfway through cooking, or until the bases are crisp and golden and the potato is tender. Serve immediately, sprinkled with a little extra rosemary.

PIZZA BIANCA CON PARMIGIANO E ROSMARINO

Parmesan cheese & rosemary pizza bread

If possible, always preheat the pizza or baking trays in the oven so that the pizzas can go straight onto hot trays. Hot, good-quality trays will result in crisp bases—just be careful when transferring the pizzas onto them before baking.

Preparation time: 10 minutes
Cooking time: 16 minutes
Makes: four 24 cm (9½ in) round pizzas (serves 8–12)

1 quantity rosemary pizza dough (see page 168)
80 ml (2½ fl oz/⅓ cup) extra virgin olive oil

50 g (1¾ oz/½ cup) finely shredded parmesan cheese
sea salt flakes, to serve

Preheat the oven to 220°C (425°F/Gas 7). Place two large, heavy pizza or baking trays in the oven to heat.

Cut the dough into four even portions and shape each into a ball. Press each ball to flatten, then use a lightly floured rolling pin to roll out each ball on a piece of non-stick baking paper to a 24 cm (9½ in) round. Make a border, pressing with your fingertips 2 cm (¾ in) from the edge. Brush the pizzas with the olive oil, sprinkle with the parmesan cheese and season with sea salt.

Remove the trays from the oven one at a time to keep them as hot as possible and carefully slide one pizza (still on the baking paper) onto each tray. Bake for 6–8 minutes, swapping the trays around halfway through cooking, or until the bases are crisp and golden. Bake the remaining two pizzas. Serve immediately.

VARIATIONS

Olive pizza bread: After making the borders, brush the pizzas with 2 tablespoons extra virgin olive oil mixed with ½ teaspoon dried oregano. Press 95 g (3¼ oz/½ cup) kalamata olives and 60 g (2¼ oz/⅓ cup) large green olives (remove the pits by placing them on a chopping board and using the heel of your hand to press down so the flesh is in large pieces) into the dough.

Semi-dried tomato & basil pizza bread: After making the borders, brush the pizzas with 2 tablespoons extra virgin olive oil, then lightly press 110 g (3¾ oz/½ cup) semi-dried (sun-blushed) tomatoes into the dough. Season with sea salt flakes. Bake the pizzas for 6 minutes, swapping the trays around halfway through cooking—be careful as the tomatoes can burn easily. Before serving, brush with 2 tablespoons extra virgin olive oil and sprinkle with 3 tablespoons small basil leaves.

Salami pizza bread

If you buy your salami from the deli counter at a store or supermarket, ask for the meat to be sliced while you wait—meat that has been cut in advance may have dried out and will look unappetising.

Preparation time: 15 minutes
Cooking time: 20 minutes
Makes: four 25 cm (10 in) round pizzas (serves 8–12)

1 quantity pizza dough (see page 168)
160 ml (5¼ fl oz/²⁄₃ cup) pizza sauce (see page 169)
150 g (5½ oz) thinly sliced salami

200 g (7 oz) fresh buffalo mozzarella cheese, thinly sliced

Preheat the oven to 230°C (450°F/Gas 8). Place two large, heavy pizza or baking trays in the oven to heat.

Cut the dough into four even portions and shape each into a ball. Press each ball to flatten, then use a lightly floured rolling pin to roll out each ball on a piece of non-stick baking paper to a 25 cm (10 in) round. Make a border, pressing with your fingertips 2 cm (¾ in) from the edge. Spread the pizzas evenly with the pizza sauce, then top with the salami and mozzarella cheese.

Remove the trays from the oven one at a time to keep them as hot as possible and carefully slide one pizza (still on the baking paper) onto each tray. Bake for 10 minutes, swapping the trays around halfway through cooking, or until crisp and golden. Bake the remaining two pizzas. Serve immediately.

FOCACCIA CON PANCETTA E PARMIGIANA

Focaccia with pancetta & parmesan cheese

One quantity of the focaccia dough (see page 171) makes two focaccia. Each of these recipes is for one focaccia, so you can make both types with one quantity of dough.

Preparation time: 10 minutes
Cooking time: 20 minutes
Makes: 1 focaccia

½ quantity focaccia dough (see page 171), rolled out
   and on a tray
90 g (3¼ oz) pancetta, diced

10 basil leaves, torn in half
olive oil, for brushing
2 tablespoons grated parmesan cheese

Preheat the oven to 220°C (425°F/Gas 7). When the dough has risen the second time, scatter the pancetta over the surface and press the pieces firmly into the focaccia dough.

Press a piece of basil into each indentation. Brush the surface of the dough with olive oil, sprinkle with parmesan cheese and bake for about 20 minutes, or until golden.

PICTURE ON OPPOSITE PAGE

FOCACCIA CON OLIVE VERDI E ROSMARINO

Focaccia with green olives & rosemary

Preparation time: 10 minutes
Cooking time: 20 minutes
Makes: 1 focaccia

½ quantity focaccia dough (see page 171), rolled out
   and on a tray
175 g (6 oz/1 cup) green olives

olive oil, for brushing
2 teaspoons coarse sea salt flakes
leaves of 2 sprigs of rosemary

Preheat the oven to 220°C (425°F/Gas 7). When the dough has risen the second time, scatter the olives over the surface and press them firmly into the focaccia dough.

Brush with olive oil and sprinkle with the sea salt and rosemary leaves. Bake for about 20 minutes, or until golden.

Pizza Quattro Stagioni

Four seasons pizza

Leave a 1 cm (½ inch) border of dough uncovered around the edge of the pizza so that the tomato paste and toppings don't drip off and burn in the oven as they heat up.

Preparation time: 10 minutes
Cooking time: 15 minutes
Makes: one 30 cm (12 in) pizza (serves 6–8)

1 x 30 cm (12 in) pizza base
cornmeal, for dusting
1 quantity pizza sauce (see page 169)
1 tablespoon grated parmesan cheese
60 g (2¼ oz) mozzarella cheese, chopped
30 g (1 oz) thinly sliced prosciutto, cut into small pieces
1 roma (plum) tomato, thinly sliced

3 basil leaves, shredded
4 small artichoke hearts, marinated in oil, drained and quartered
4 button mushrooms, sliced
pinch of dried oregano
1 tablespoon olive oil

Preheat the oven to 240°C (475°F/Gas 9). Put the pizza base on a baking tray dusted with cornmeal. Spoon the tomato sauce onto the base, spreading it to within 1 cm (½ inch) of the the rim. Sprinkle the parmesan cheese on top.

Visually divide the pizza into quarters and scatter the mozzarella cheese over two of the opposite quarters. Spread the prosciutto pieces over one

of these, and arrange the tomato slices over the other. Lightly salt the tomato and sprinkle on the basil. Arrange the artichoke quarters over the third quarter, and the mushrooms over the final quarter. Sprinkle the oregano over both these sections.

Drizzle the olive oil over the pizza and bake for 12–15 minutes, or until golden and puffed.

PIZZA TURCA

Turkish pizza

Preparation time: 120 minutes (+ cooling time)
Cooking time: 45 minutes
Makes: eight 12 x 18 cm (4½ x 7 in) oval pizzas (serves 8)

60 ml (2 fl oz/¼ cup) olive oil, plus extra, for greasing
1 brown onion, finely chopped
500 g (1 lb 2 oz) minced (ground) lamb
2 garlic cloves, crushed
1 teaspoon ground cinnamon
1½ teaspoons ground cumin
½ teaspoon cayenne pepper

60 g (2¼ oz/¼ cup) tomato paste (concentrated purée)
400 g (14 oz) tinned chopped tomatoes
50 g (1¾ oz/⅓ cup) pine nuts
2 tablespoons chopped coriander (cilantro) leaves
1 quantity pizza dough (see page 168)
Greek-style yoghurt, coriander (cilantro) leaves and
    lemon cheeks, to serve

Heat 2 tablespoons of the olive oil in a frying
pan over medium–high heat. Cook the onion
for 5 minutes, or until soft but not golden. Add
the lamb and cook, breaking up with a wooden
spoon, for 10 minutes or until brown. Add the
garlic, spices, tomato paste and tomatoes. Cook for
15 minutes, stirring occasionally, until reduced to
a thick sauce. Add half the pine nuts and the
chopped coriander. Season with salt and freshly
ground black pepper. Transfer to a bowl and place
in the refrigerator until cooled to room temperature.

Preheat the oven to 210°C (415°F/Gas 6–7).
Lightly grease three large, heavy baking trays
with olive oil.

Cut the dough into eight even portions and shape
each into a ball. Press each ball to flatten, then use
a lightly floured rolling pin to roll out each ball
on a lightly floured surface to a 12 x 18 cm
(4½ x 7 in) oval. Place the pizzas on the trays,
spacing evenly. Divide the lamb mixture evenly
among the pizzas and spread, leaving a 3 cm (1¼ in)
border. Sprinkle with the remaining pine nuts.
Brush the edges with a little water. Fold the border
up at the edges to contain the filling and then
pinch the ends together to form a boat shape.
Brush the edges with the remaining olive oil.

Bake the pizzas for 15 minutes, swapping the trays
around halfway through cooking, or until golden
and cooked through. Serve immediately, topped
with the yoghurt and coriander, and accompanied
by the lemon cheeks.

SALUMI

⋄⋄⋄⋄⋄⋄⋄⋄⋄⋄⋄⋄⋄⋄⋄⋄⋄⋄⋄⋄⋄⋄⋄⋄⋄⋄⋄⋄⋄⋄⋄⋄⋄⋄⋄⋄

Salumi is the term used to refer to all Italy's cured or preserved pork products, from salami and salsicce *(sausages) to cured hams such as Parma, cooked hams such as* prosciutto cotto, *and ingredients from lard to pancetta and* coppa.

Curing meat was once the only way in which meat could be enjoyed year round. A family would keep a pig to be butchered in the winter, then turn it into *salumi* to be eaten throughout the year. Though beef, wild boar and venison are used for making cured meats, pork has always predominated, made popular by the fact that every scrap of the animal can be used. When the pig was butchered, the fat would be rendered into lard, the best meat turned into hams and pancetta, the rest of the pig used to make salami and sausages, and the bones saved for stock. The meats would then be cured, usually by drying, smoking or preserving in fat. In Italy, you can still buy just about every part of the pig, including *guanciale*, cured pig's cheek; trotters, boned and stuffed to make *zampone*; and the neck, cured and made into *coppa*.

Norcia in Umbria is renowned for its pork butchers and the town gives its name to *norcini*, which is a term used throughout Italy to mean pork butchers. *Norcini* from this area traditionally travelled all over Italy during the butchering and curing season in November to ply their trade, returning home in April. Butcher shops in central Italy that specialise in local cured pork and wild boar products are known as *norcineria*.

In Italy, butchers display their salami marked as pork (*suino*) or beef (*bovino*), and some may be labelled *salsicce* rather than salami. A salami can be sold under its own name or marked '*nostrano*', meaning that it is from the area or home-made. Salami change in flavour and texture according to where they are made. The Northeast tends towards heavier, more Austrian-tasting salami, the Centre prefers a more refined texture, while in the South salami are often spicy. Flavourings may also be added to standard salami—in Tuscany this is often fennel seed and in Umbria truffles are used. The larger the salami, the thinner it should be sliced.

Prosciutto crudo is a cured ham made from an air-dried pig's leg and sliced paper-thin for antipasto. Parma ham is just one type of prosciutto and many regions produce their own hams. *Prosciutto salato*, salted hams, are cured heavily with salt. Tuscan ham is one of the finest and these robust hams can be excellent eaten with unsalted bread. Parma and San Daniele hams are both *prosciutto dolce*, sweet hams, whose subtle curing and longer hanging give them a sweet, refined flavour.

Ham, spinach & ricotta calzone

Using grated pecorino (made from sheep's milk) will give this calzone a slightly stronger and a saltier taste than if you use the parmesan cheese (made from cow's milk). Authentic Italian parmesan cheese, known as Parmigiano Reggiano, always has branding on the rind.

Preparation time: 20 minutes
Cooking time: 20 minutes
Makes: two large calzone (serves 4)

550 g (1 lb 4 oz) firm, fresh ricotta cheese
½ teaspoon freshly grated nutmeg
250 g (9 oz) leg ham, finely chopped
120 g (4¼ oz) finely grated pecorino or parmesan cheese

100 g (3½ oz) baby English spinach leaves, roughly
  chopped
1 quantity pizza dough (see page 168)

Combine the ricotta, nutmeg, ham and pecorino or parmesan cheese in a large bowl and season with salt and freshly ground black pepper. Add the spinach and stir to combine.

Preheat the oven to 220°C (425°F/Gas 7).

Cut the dough into two even portions and shape each into a ball. Press each ball to flatten, then use a lightly floured rolling pin to roll out each ball on a piece of non-stick baking paper to a 30 cm (12 in) round. Transfer the dough rounds (still on the baking paper) to two large, heavy baking trays.

Divide the ham mixture between the dough rounds, spreading it evenly over one half only and leaving a 1.5 cm (⅝ in) border around the edges. Use a pastry brush or your fingertips to lightly brush the borders with water. Fold the uncovered half of each dough round up and over the filling, then press the edges firmly together in a fluted pattern to seal.

Bake for 15–20 minutes, swapping the trays around halfway through cooking, or until golden and cooked through. Serve immediately in slices.

Pepperoni pizza

You can replace the pepperoni sausage with 150 g (5½ oz) fresh pork and fennel sausage. Thinly sliced, unsmoked, streaky bacon slices will make a suitable substitute for the pancetta.

Preparation time: 15 minutes
Cooking time: 15 minutes
Makes: two 34 cm (13½ in) round pizzas (serves 4)

1 quantity pizza dough (see page 168)
1 quantity pizza sauce (see page 169)
250 g (9 oz) fresh buffalo mozzarella cheese,
   thinly sliced

150 g (5½ oz) pepperoni sausage, thinly sliced
100 g (3½ oz) salami, thinly sliced
100 g (3½ oz) thinly sliced pancetta, roughly torn
mixed leaf salad, to serve

Preheat the oven to 220°C (425°F/Gas 7). Place two large, heavy pizza or baking trays in the oven to heat.

Cut the dough into two even portions and shape each into a ball. Press each ball to flatten, then use a lightly floured rolling pin to roll out each ball on a piece of non-stick baking paper to a 34 cm (13½ in) round. Spread the pizzas evenly with the pizza sauce, then top with the mozzarella cheese, pepperoni, salami and pancetta.

Remove the trays from the oven one at a time to keep them as hot as possible and carefully slide one pizza (still on the baking paper) onto each tray. Bake for 15 minutes, swapping the trays around halfway through cooking, or until the bases are crisp and golden and the mozzarella cheese is bubbling. Serve immediately, accompanied by a mixed leaf salad.

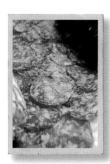

PIZZA AI QUATTRO FORMAGGI

Four cheese pizza

Many ricottas are produced from the whey that is drained off in the making of cheeses such as mozzarella cheese and provolone cheese. Because of this, technically, ricotta is not a cheese because it is made from a cheese by-product.

Preparation time: 5 minutes
Cooking time: 20 minutes
Makes: four 25 cm (10 in) round pizzas (serves 4)

1 quantity pizza dough (see page 168)
olive oil, for drizzling
150 g (5½ oz) bocconcini (fresh baby mozzarella cheese), thinly sliced, drained on paper towel

120 g (4¼ oz) firm, fresh ricotta cheese
100 g (3½ oz) blue cheese, sliced
80 g (2¾ oz) finely grated parmesan cheese

Preheat the oven to 230°C (450°F/Gas 8). Place two large, heavy pizza or baking trays in the oven to heat.

Cut the dough into four even portions and shape each into a ball. Press each ball to flatten, then use a lightly floured rolling pin to roll out each ball on a piece of non-stick baking paper to a 25 cm (10 in) round. Make a border, pressing with your fingertips 2 cm (¾ in) from the edge.

Drizzle the pizzas with olive oil and top with the bocconcini. Crumble over the ricotta and blue cheese then sprinkle with the parmesan cheese.

Remove the trays from the oven one at a time to keep them as hot as possible and carefully slide one pizza (still on the baking paper) onto each tray. Bake for 10 minutes, swapping the trays around halfway through cooking, until the bases are crisp and golden. Bake the remaining two pizzas. Serve immediately.

PISSALADÉRE

Onion & anchovy tart

Pissaladière takes its name from *pissalat*, puréed anchovies. It can vary in its topping, from onions and anchovies to onions, tomatoes and anchovies, or simply anchovies puréed with garlic. The dough used is usually a bread dough, which is thicker than that of the classic pizza

Preparation time: 10 minutes
Cooking time: 65 minutes
Makes: one 34 x 26 cm (13½ x 10½ in) rectangle tart (serves 6)

40 g (1½ oz) butter
2 tablespoons olive oil
1.5 kg (3 lb 6 oz) onions, thinly sliced
2 tablespoons thyme leaves

1 quantity bread dough (page 170)
16 anchovies, halved lengthways
24 pitted olives

Melt the butter with half the oil in a saucepan and add the onion and half the thyme. Cover and cook over low heat, stirring occasionally, for 45 minutes, or until the onion is softened but not browned. Season and set aside to cool.

Preheat the oven to 200°C (400°F/Gas 6). Roll out the bread dough to roughly fit an oiled 34 x 26 cm (13½ x 10½ in) shallow baking tray. Brush with the remaining oil, then spread with the onion.

Lay the anchovies in a lattice pattern over the top of the onion and arrange the olives in the lattice diamonds.

Bake for 20 minutes, or until the dough is cooked and lightly browned. Sprinkle with the remaining thyme leaves and cut into squares. Serve hot or warm.

Far left: Spread the softened onion over the bread base.

Left: Arrange the anchovies over the top in the traditional lattice pattern.

Chapter 2

CONTEMPORARY

Contemporary pizzas are perfect for anyone looking for fresh and flavoursome pizzas with a difference. The addition of a few unexpected toppings and a handful of spices transforms the taste but keeps the pizza simple to prepare and delicious to eat.

Mini caramelised fennel, fig & prosciutto pizzas with rocket pesto

Native to the Mediterranean but now widely grown, fennel is cultivated for its aromatic leaves and seeds, similar in flavour to aniseed. Its thick stems and bulbous base can be eaten raw like celery.

Preparation time: 20 minutes
Cooking time: 27 minutes
Makes: 15 mini round pizzas

2 teaspoons olive oil
2 fennel bulbs (about 200 g/7 oz each), trimmed,
   thinly sliced
½ teaspoon lemon juice
2 garlic cloves, crushed

1 quantity pizza dough (see page 168)
150 g (5½ oz/¾ cup) rocket pesto (see page 173)
4 firm, ripe figs, sliced lengthways
120 g (4¼ oz) soft goat's cheese, coarsely crumbled
100 g (3½ oz) thinly sliced prosciutto, torn into pieces

Heat the olive oil in a large non-stick frying pan over low heat. Add the fennel and lemon juice and cook, stirring occasionally, for 15 minutes or until starting to colour and caramelise. Add the garlic and cook for 2 minutes. Remove from the heat and season with salt and freshly ground black pepper.

Preheat the oven to 230°C (450°F/Gas 8). Line three large, heavy baking trays with non-stick baking paper.

Cut the dough into 15 even portions and shape each into a ball. Press each ball to flatten, then use a lightly floured rolling pin to roll out each ball on a lightly floured surface to a 9 cm (3½ in) round. Place the pizzas on the trays, leaving 3 cm (1¼ in) between each.

Spread the pizzas with half the rocket pesto, then top with the caramelised fennel, a fig slice and some goat's cheese.

Bake the pizzas for 10 minutes, swapping the trays around halfway through cooking, or until the bases are crisp and golden.

Serve the pizzas immediately, topped with the prosciutto and the remaining pesto.

Potato, onion & salami calzone
Mozzarella cheese & prosciutto calzone

A calzone is a half-moon shaped pizza. The dough is rolled into a thin oval shape, one half is filled, then the dough is folded and sealed.

Preparation time: 20 minutes
Cooking time: 20 minutes
Makes: two calzone (serves 4)

1 quantity pizza dough (see page 168)

POTATO, ONION & SALAMI CALZONE
2 tablespoons vegetable oil
cornmeal, for dusting
1 small onion, very thinly sliced
75 g (2½ oz) small red potatoes, unpeeled,
　very thinly sliced
75 g (2½ oz) mozzarella cheese, cut into
　2 cm (¾ in) cubes

60 g (2¼ oz) sliced salami
2 tablespoons grated parmesan cheese

MOZZARELLA CHEESE & PROSCIUTTO CALZONE
170 g (6 oz) mozzarella cheese, cut into
　2 cm (¾ in) cubes
2 thin slices prosciutto, cut in half
1 artichoke heart, marinated in oil, drained and cut into
　3 slices from top to bottom

Preheat the oven to 230°C (450°F/Gas 8). Lightly oil a baking tray and dust with cornmeal. On a lightly floured surface, roll out the dough to form an 18 cm (7 in) circle. Using the heels of your hands and working from the centre outwards, press the circle out to a diameter of about 30 cm (12 in). Transfer to the baking tray. Lightly brush the entire surface with the oil.

To make the potato, onion and salami calzone, heat the oil in a frying pan and add the onion. Cook for 1 minute, then scatter the potato on top. Cook, stirring, for 3–4 minutes, until beginning to brown. Season, then spread over half of the dough circle, leaving a narrow border around the edge. Scatter with the mozzarella cheese, followed by the salami slices and parmesan cheese.

Fold the other side of the circle over the filling to make a half-moon shape. Match the cut edges and

press firmly together. Fold them over and press into a scrolled pattern to thoroughly seal in the filling. Brush the surface with a little extra olive oil, then transfer to the oven. Bake for about 20 minutes, or until the crust is golden.

To make the mozzarella cheese and prosciutto calzone, spread the mozzarella cheese over half of the dough circle, leaving a narrow border around the edge. Roll the prosciutto into little tubes and arrange on top of the cheese. Top with the artichoke slices and season to taste.

Fold the other side of the circle over the filling to make a half-moon shape. Match the cut edges and press firmly together. Fold them over and press into a scrolled pattern to thoroughly seal in the filling. Brush the surface with a little extra olive oil, then transfer to the oven. Bake for about 20 minutes, or until the crust is golden.

Tarte flambée

Flamed tart

Tarte flambée is the Alsatian version of the pizza. It is cooked quickly at a very high temperature in a wood-fired oven and takes its name from the fact that the edge of the dough often caught fire in the intense heat of the oven.

Preparation time: 10 minutes
Cooking time: 10–15 minutes
Makes: one 34 x 26 cm (13½ x 10½ in) rectangle tart (serves 6)

2 tablespoons olive oil
2 white onions, sliced
100 g (3½ oz) cream or curd cheese

185 g (6½ oz/¾ cup) fromage frais
200 g (7 oz) piece of bacon, cut into small strips
1 quantity bread dough (page 170)

Preheat the oven to 230°C (450°F/Gas 8). Heat the olive oil in a saucepan and fry the onion until softened but not browned.

Beat the cream or curd cheese with the fromage frais and then add the onion and bacon strips and season to taste

Roll out the bread dough into a rectangle about 3 mm (⅛ in) thick—the dough needs to be thin—and place on an oiled baking tray. Fold the edge of the dough over to make a slight rim. Spread the topping over the dough, right up to the rim, and bake for 10–15 minutes, or until the dough is crisp and cooked and the topping browned. Cut into squares to serve.

Pizza con trota e zucchine

Ocean trout & zucchini pizza

Zucchini (courgettes) are baby marrows, usually dark green in colour but there are also light green and yellow varieties. Buy and eat quickly as storage in the fridge makes the texture deteriorate.

Preparation time: 20 minutes
Cooking time: 22 minutes
Makes: four 24 cm (9½ in) round pizzas (serves 4)

1 quantity pizza dough (see page 168)
185 g (6½ oz/¾ cup) sour cream
60 g (2¼ oz/¼ cup) firm, fresh ricotta cheese
finely grated zest of 2 lemons
2 zucchini (courgettes), very thinly sliced on the diagonal
1 lemon, very thinly sliced
500 g (1 lb 2 oz) skinless ocean trout fillets,
  cut into 3–4 mm (⅛ in) slices

HERB SALAD
1 tablespoon lemon juice
1½ tablespoons extra virgin olive oil
1 small handful dill sprigs
1 handful chives snipped into 3 cm (1¼ in) lengths
1½ tablespoons baby capers in brine, rinsed, drained

Preheat the oven to 230°C (450°F/Gas 8). Place two large, heavy pizza or baking trays in the oven to heat.

Cut the dough into four even portions and shape each into a ball. Press each ball to flatten, then use a lightly floured rolling pin to roll out each ball on a piece of non-stick baking paper to a 24 cm (9½ in) round. Make a border, pressing with your fingertips 2 cm (¾ in) from the edge.

Combine the sour cream, ricotta, lemon zest and salt and freshly ground black pepper, to taste. Spread a thin layer of the sour cream mixture over each pizza. Top with the zucchini and lemon slices.

Remove the trays from the oven one at a time to keep them as hot as possible and carefully slide one pizza (still on the baking paper) onto each tray. Bake for 8 minutes. Remove the pizzas from the oven and top with half the trout slices. Return pizzas to the oven, swapping the trays around, and bake for a further 2–3 minutes or until the bases are crisp and golden. Repeat with the remaining two pizzas and trout.

Meanwhile, for the herb salad, combine all the ingredients in a bowl, season with salt and freshly ground black pepper and toss gently. Serve the pizzas immediately, topped with the herb salad.

PIZZA BIANCA SPAGNOLA

Spanish pizza bread

This pizza has a thicker base than traditional Italian pizzas. The onion and olives add a rich flavour. Black olives are the same fruit as green olives but are picked half ripe (purple) or fully ripe (black) and then cured. Varieties include kalamata and Niçoise.

Preparation time: 10 minutes
Cooking time: 45–50 minutes
Makes: one 25 x 30 cm (10 x 12 in) pizza bread (serves 4–6)

1 tablespoon olive oil, plus extra, for greasing
2 bunches English spinach leaves, washed,
   drained, shredded
2 brown onions, chopped
2 garlic cloves, crushed

400 g (14 oz) tinned whole tomatoes, drained, crushed
¼ teaspoon freshly ground black pepper
1 quantity pizza dough (see page 168)
100 g (3½ oz/⅔ cup) roughly chopped, pitted
   black olives

Preheat the oven to 210°C (415°F/Gas 6–7). Grease a 25 x 30 cm (10 x 12 in) Swiss roll (jelly roll) tin with olive oil.

To make the topping, cook the spinach in a large saucepan over low heat, stirring occasionally, for 3–5 minutes or until wilted and the excess water evaporates. Drain the spinach well and set aside to cool. Once cool enough to handle, use your hands to squeeze out any excess moisture from the spinach. Set aside.

Heat the oil in the cleaned saucepan over medium–low heat. Cook the onion and garlic for

8 minutes, or until softened. Add the tomatoes and pepper and simmer gently, stirring occasionally for 5 minutes or until thickened.

On a lightly floured surface, use a lightly floured rolling pin to roll out the pizza dough to the same size as the tin. Place the pizza in the tin. Spread with the wilted spinach, top with the tomato mixture and sprinkle with the olives.

Bake the pizza bread for 25–30 minutes or until the base is golden and cooked through. Serve warm or at room temperature.

Chilli vongole pizza

Clams can be either soft or hard shelled. Hard-shelled clams come in different sizes and colours, and can be clam shaped or like long razors. Clams must be bought live, then shucked and cleaned before use.

Preparation time: 10 minutes
Cooking time: 25 minutes
Makes: four 24 cm (9½ in) round pizzas (serves 4)

1 kg (2 lb 4 oz) clams (vongole), washed
1 quantity pizza dough (see page 168)
1 quantity tomato & chilli pizza sauce (see page 169)
200 g (7 oz) bocconcini (fresh baby mozzarella cheese), thinly sliced, drained on paper towel

2 garlic cloves, thinly sliced
2 tablespoons chopped flat-leaf (Italian) parsley
finely grated zest of 1 lemon
1 tablespoon extra virgin olive oil

Place the clams in a large, deep frying pan or saucepan with 1.5 cm (⅝ in) of water over medium heat. Bring to a simmer and remove the clams with tongs as they open. Discard any unopened clams. Remove half of the clams completely from their shells. (If you are using larger clams, leave the other half in their shells but remove the top shell.) Set aside to cool.

Preheat the oven to 230°C (450°F/Gas 8). Place two large, heavy pizza or baking trays in the oven to heat.

Cut the dough into four even portions and shape each into a ball. Press each ball to flatten, then use a lightly floured rolling pin to roll out each ball on a piece of non-stick baking paper to a

24 cm (9½ in) round. Spread the pizzas evenly with the pizza sauce, then top with half the bocconcini, the garlic, parsley and lemon zest. Top with the remaining bocconcini. Drizzle with the extra virgin olive oil and season with salt and freshly ground black pepper.

Remove the trays from the oven one at a time to keep them as hot as possible and carefully slide one pizza (still on the baking paper) onto each tray. Bake for 7 minutes. Remove the pizzas from the oven and top with half the shelled and unshelled clams. Return the pizzas to the oven, swapping the trays around, and bake for a further 3–4 minutes, or until the bases are crisp and golden. Repeat with the remaining two pizzas and clams. Serve immediately.

PIZZA CON POLLO, PARMIGIANO E GREMOLATA
Chicken & parmesan cheese gremolata pizza

Preparation time: 15 minutes
Cooking time: 25 minutes
Makes: four 23 cm (9 in) square pizzas (serves 4)

400 g (14 oz) boneless, skinless chicken breasts,
   cut across the grain, thinly sliced
4 garlic cloves, finely chopped
finely grated zest of 2 lemons
20 g (¾ oz) finely chopped flat-leaf (Italian) parsley
70 g (2½ oz/½ cup) finely grated parmesan cheese

1 quantity pizza dough (see page 168)
1 quantity pizza sauce (see page 169)
280 g (10 oz) fresh buffalo mozzarella cheese, thinly
   sliced
120 g (4¼ oz/½ cup) whole-egg mayonnaise

Preheat the oven to 230°C (450°F/Gas 8). Place
two large, heavy baking trays in the oven to heat.

Combine the chicken, garlic, lemon zest, parsley,
parmesan cheese and salt and freshly ground black
pepper, to taste, in a bowl and stir well to coat
the chicken.

Cut the dough into four even portions and shape
each into a ball. Press each ball to flatten, then
use a lightly floured rolling pin to roll out each
ball on a piece of non-stick baking paper to a
23 cm (9 in) square. Make a border, pressing with
your fingertips 2 cm (¾ in) from the edge.

Spread the pizzas with the pizza sauce, top
with the mozzarella cheese and then top with
the chicken mixture.

Remove the trays from the oven one at a time to
keep them as hot as possible and carefully slide
one pizza (still on the baking paper) onto each tray.
Bake for 10–12 minutes, swapping the trays around
halfway through cooking, or until the bases are
crisp and golden. Bake the remaining two pizzas.

Meanwhile, thin the mayonnaise with a little water.
Serve the pizzas immediately, drizzled with the
mayonnaise.

Ham & pineapple pizza

If you have a block of mozzarella cheese which you need to grate, place it in the freezer for 20 minutes before you use it. The texture will become firmer and the cheese will be much easier to grate.

Preparation time: 15 minutes
Cooking time: 20 minutes
Makes: four 25 cm (10 in) round pizzas (serves 4)

1 quantity pizza dough (see page 168)
160 ml (5¼ fl oz/⅔ cup) pizza sauce (see page 169)
320 g (11¼ oz) fresh pineapple, cut into small, thin wedges
200 g (7 oz) leg ham, chopped

125 g (4½ oz/1 cup) coarsely grated mozzarella cheese
basil leaves (optional), to garnish

Preheat the oven to 230°C (450°F/Gas 8). Place two large, heavy pizza or baking trays in the oven to heat.

Cut the dough into four even portions and shape each into a ball. Press each ball to flatten, then use a lightly floured rolling pin to roll out each ball on a piece of non-stick baking paper to a 25 cm (10 in) round.

Spread the pizzas evenly with the pizza sauce, then top with the pineapple, ham and mozzarella cheese.

Remove the trays from the oven one at a time to keep them as hot as possible and carefully slide one pizza (still on the baking paper) onto each tray. Bake for 10 minutes, swapping the trays around halfway through cooking, or until the bases are crisp and golden. Bake the remaining two pizzas. Serve immediately, sprinkled with the basil, if using.

Cauliflower & pine nut pizza

Tahini is a Middle Eastern paste made from ground sesame seeds. Look for it in the health-food section of your supermarket.

Preparation time: 20 minutes
Cooking time: 35–40 minutes
Makes: four 25 cm (10 in) round pizzas (serves 4)

1 tablespoon olive oil
800 g (1 lb 12 oz) cauliflower, cut into small florets
1 quantity parmesan cheese pizza dough (see page 168)
150 g (5½ oz) coarsely grated mozzarella cheese
2 tablespoons currants
50 g (1¾ oz/⅓ cup) pine nuts

70 g (2½ oz/¼ cup) Greek-style yoghurt
1 tablespoon tahini
1 tablespoon lemon juice
2 tablespoons chopped flat-leaf (Italian) parsley, to garnish

Heat the olive oil in a large non-stick frying pan over high heat. Add the cauliflower and cook, stirring occasionally, for 5–6 minutes or until golden and just tender. Remove from the heat and season with salt and freshly ground black pepper.

Preheat the oven to 230°C (450°F/Gas 8). Place two large, heavy pizza or baking trays in the oven to heat.

Cut the dough into four even portions and shape each into a ball. Press each ball to flatten, then use a lightly floured rolling pin to roll out each ball on a piece of non-stick baking paper to a 25 cm (10 in) round.

Top the pizzas with half the mozzarella cheese, the cauliflower and currants, then sprinkle with the remaining mozzarella cheese.

Remove the trays from the oven one at a time to keep them as hot as possible and carefully slide one pizza (still on the baking paper) onto each tray. Bake for 5 minutes. Remove the pizzas from the oven and sprinkle with half the pine nuts. Return the pizzas to the oven, swapping the trays around, and bake for a further 10 minutes, or until the bases are crisp and golden. Repeat with the remaining two pizzas and pine nuts.

Meanwhile, combine the yoghurt, tahini and lemon juice in a bowl. Add 1–2 tablespoons of water to thin to the desired consistency.

Serve the pizzas immediately, drizzled with the tahini dressing and sprinkled with the parsley.

Pizza con ricotta, spinaci e pancetta

Ricotta, spinach & bacon pizza pie

Oregano is traditionally used to flavour tomato sauces in Italian cooking and is usually used dried. Oregano has a strong flavour and should be used sparingly.

Preparation time: 25 minutes
Cooking time: 35 minutes
Makes: one 24 cm (9½ in) pie (serves 6–8)

2 teaspoons olive oil, plus extra, for greasing
   and brushing
1 large brown onion, chopped
175 g (6 oz) bacon, trimmed of most of the fat,
   roughly chopped
1 quantity parmesan cheese pizza dough (see page 168)
1 bunch English spinach (about 280 g/10 oz), trimmed,
   washed, drained

250 g (9 oz) firm, fresh ricotta cheese
1 small handful finely snipped chives
1 small handful oregano leaves
finely grated zest of ½ lemon
1 egg
100 g (3½ oz/²/₃ cup) crumbled feta cheese
1 quantity roasted tomato pizza sauce (see page 169),
   to serve

Preheat the oven to 230°C (450°F/Gas 8). Grease a 24 cm (9½ in) springform cake tin with oil.

Heat the olive oil in a large frying pan over medium heat and cook the onion and bacon, stirring occasionally, for 5 minutes or until the onion softens. Increase the heat to high and cook for another 1–2 minutes to give a little colour. Transfer to a plate and set aside to cool.

Meanwhile, add the spinach to a saucepan of salted boiling water and cook for 1 minute, or until just wilted and bright green. Drain and place in iced water to refresh. Drain and then use your hands to squeeze out the water. Place the spinach on a clean tea towel (dish towel) and roll and squeeze to extract any excess moisture. Roughly chop the spinach.

In a bowl, combined the spinach, bacon and onion mixture with the ricotta, chives, oregano, lemon zest and egg. Season with salt and freshly ground black pepper. Mix well to combine. Gently stir through the feta.

Shape two-thirds of the dough into a ball. Press to flatten, then use a lightly floured rolling pin to roll out on a lightly floured surface to a 36 cm (14¼ in) round. Shape the remaining dough into a ball and then roll out to a 28 cm (11¼ in) round. Line the base of the tin with the larger round, pressing it into the base and corners and bringing it about 6 cm (2½ in) up the side of the tin. Spoon the filling into the tin and smooth the surface. Brush the rim of the dough lightly with water. Place the remaining round on top. Fold over the edges to seal. Brush the top with olive oil.

Bake for 25 minutes, or until golden and cooked through. Cool in the tin for 5 minutes. Serve warm or at room temperature with the pizza sauce.

Chorizo, rosemary, mushroom & rocket pizza

You can use thinly sliced pepperoni instead of the chorizo, if you like. Pizza cheese is a pre-grated cheese made up of a combination of mozzarella, parmesan and cheddar which is available in many supermarkets.

Preparation time: 15 minutes
Cooking time: 20 minutes
Makes: four 25 cm (10 in) round pizzas (serves 2–4)

1 quantity pizza dough (see page 168)
160 g (5¾ oz/²/₃ cup) semi-dried tomato tapenade
   (see page 172)
150 g (5½ oz) button mushrooms, thinly sliced
1 chorizo (about 150 g/5½ oz), thinly sliced

2 teaspoons chopped rosemary
160 g (5¾ oz) coarsely grated pizza cheese
80 g (2¾ oz) rocket (arugula) leaves
1 tablespoon balsamic vinegar

Preheat the oven to 220°C (425°F/Gas 7). Place two large, heavy pizza or baking trays in the oven to heat.

Cut the dough into four even portions and shape each into a ball. Press each ball to flatten, then use a lightly floured rolling pin to roll out each ball on a piece of non-stick baking paper to a 25 cm (10 in) round. Spread the pizzas with the tapenade, then top with the mushrooms, chorizo, rosemary and pizza cheese.

Remove the trays from the oven one at a time to keep them as hot as possible and carefully slide one pizza (still on the baking paper) onto each tray. Bake for 10 minutes, swapping trays halfway through cooking, or until the bases are crisp and golden. Bake the remaining two pizzas.

Meanwhile, place the rocket in a medium bowl, drizzle with the balsamic and toss to combine. Serve the pizzas immediately, topped with the dressed rocket.

Haloumi, chilli, prawn & cherry tomato pizza

Haloumi is the perfect cheese for using as a topping because it retains its shape and will not melt. Some brands are very salty so ask to try a sample before you buy.

Preparation time: 20 minutes
Cooking time: 16 minutes
Makes: two 20 x 35 cm (8 x 14 in) rectangle pizzas (serves 4)

2 tablespoons olive oil
200 g (7 oz) haloumi cheese, thinly sliced
1 quantity pizza dough (see page 168), made using
    2 tablespoons finely chopped oregano when
    adding the olive oil

800 g (1 lb 12 oz) raw prawns (shrimp), peeled,
    deveined, tails left intact
125 ml (4 fl oz/½ cup) tomato & chilli pizza sauce
    (see page 169)
250 g (9 oz) cherry tomatoes, halved
oregano leaves, to garnish

Preheat the oven to 230°C (450°F/Gas 8). Place two large, heavy baking trays in the oven to heat.

Heat 1 tablespoon of the olive oil in a large frying pan over medium–high heat until hot. Add half the haloumi and cook for 2–3 minutes, turning once, or until golden. Remove from the pan and repeat with the remaining haloumi. Set aside.

Cut the dough into two even portions and shape each into a ball. Press each ball to flatten, then use a lightly floured rolling pin to roll out each ball on a piece of non-stick baking paper to a 20 x 35 cm (8 x 14 in) rectangle.

Toss the prawns with the remaining olive oil. Spread the bases with the pizza sauce, then top with the tomatoes, prawns and haloumi.

Remove the trays from the oven one at a time to keep them as hot as possible and carefully slide one pizza (still on the baking paper) onto each tray. Bake for 10 minutes, swapping the trays around halfway through cooking, or until the bases are golden and crisp. Serve immediately, sprinkled with the oregano.

Sardine & silverbeet wholemeal pizza

Preparation time: 20 minutes (+ 10 minutes draining time)
Cooking time: 32 minutes
Makes: two 30 cm (12 in) round pizzas (serves 4)

2½ tablespoons extra virgin olive oil
1 large brown onion, finely chopped
5 garlic cloves, thinly sliced
1 bunch silverbeet (Swiss chard), stems removed,
 leaves washed, dried, roughly chopped
120 g (4¼ oz/²/₃ cup) raisins, roughly chopped
150 g (5½ oz/1½ cups) finely grated
 parmesan cheese

large pinch of chilli flakes, or to taste
1 quantity wholemeal pizza dough (see page 168)
210 g (7 oz) tinned sardines in oil, drained,
 halved lengthways
finely grated parmesan cheese (optional), to serve

Heat the oil in a large saucepan over medium–high heat. Cook the onion for 6–8 minutes, or until soft and starting to colour. Add the garlic and cook for 30 seconds or until aromatic. Add the silverbeet and raisins, cover, then cook for 3 minutes, stirring often, or until the silverbeet wilts. Transfer the mixture to a colander and set aside for 10 minutes to drain. Use your hands to squeeze out excess moisture then place in a bowl. Stir in the parmesan cheese, chilli, and salt and freshly ground black pepper.

Preheat the oven to 220°C (425°F/Gas 7). Place two large, heavy pizza or baking trays in the oven to heat.

Cut the dough into two even portions and shape each into a ball. Press each ball to flatten, then use a lightly floured rolling pin to roll out each ball on a piece of non-stick baking paper to a 30 cm (12 in) round. Divide the silverbeet mixture between the bases, scattering to cover, then arrange the sardines on top.

Remove the trays from the oven one at a time to keep them as hot as possible and carefully slide one pizza (still on the baking paper) onto each tray. Bake the pizzas for 18–20 minutes, swapping the trays around halfway through cooking, or until the bases are crisp and golden. Serve immediately, sprinkled with the parmesan cheese, if using.

Individual salami & ham calzone

Preparation time: 20 minutes
Cooking time: 12–15 minutes
Makes: four calzone (serves 4)

1 quantity wholemeal pizza dough (see page 168)
125 ml (4 fl oz/½ cup) pizza sauce (see page 169)
160 g (5¾ oz/1¼ cups) coarsely grated mozzarella
cheese
100 g (3½ oz) piece of salami, cut into 1 cm (½ in)
cubes

100 g (3½ oz) leg ham, chopped
4 eggs, lightly beaten
1 tablespoon chopped flat-leaf (Italian) parsley
100 g (3½ oz) firm, fresh ricotta cheese
2 teaspoons olive oil
2 tablespoons finely grated parmesan cheese

Preheat the oven to 230°C (450°F/Gas 8). Place two large, heavy pizza or baking trays in the oven to heat.

Cut the dough into four even portions and shape each into a ball. Press each ball to flatten, then use a lightly floured rolling pin to roll out each ball on a piece of non-stick baking paper to a 25 cm (10 in) round.

Spread the dough rounds evenly with the pizza sauce. Place the mozzarella cheese, salami and ham in a bowl, add the egg, parsley, and salt and freshly ground black pepper, to taste, and stir to combine. Break the ricotta into large pieces over the top and gently stir to combine.

Divide the salami mixture among the dough rounds, piling it evenly over one half only. Use a pastry brush to lightly brush the borders with the olive oil. Fold the uncovered half of each dough round up and over the filling, then press the edges together to seal well.

Remove the trays from the oven one at a time to keep them as hot as possible and carefully slide two calzone (still on the baking paper) onto each tray. Sprinkle the tops of the calzone with the parmesan cheese. Bake for 12–15 minutes, swapping the trays around halfway through cooking, or until the dough is crisp and golden. Cool for 2–3 minutes before serving.

Lamb & rosemary pizza

Use tongs to turn the lamb steaks as piercing the meat with a fork will drain the juices from the lamb. Use the blunt end of the tongs to prod the meat in the thickest part of the steak to check if the lamb is properly cooked.

Preparation time: 10 minutes
Cooking time: 28 minutes
Makes: four 25 cm (10 in) round pizzas (serves 4)

olive oil, for brushing
300 g (10½ oz) haloumi cheese, thinly sliced
1 quantity rosemary pizza dough (see page 168)
1 quantity semi-dried tomato tapenade (see page 172)

500 g (1 lb 2 oz) lamb leg steaks (1 cm/½ in thick)
1 quantity mint & chilli pesto (see page 173)
1 small handful flat-leaf (Italian) parsley leaves
lemon wedges, to serve

Preheat the oven to 230°C (425°F/Gas 7). Place two large, heavy pizza or baking trays in the oven to heat.

Brush a chargrill pan with olive oil and heat over medium–high heat. Add the haloumi and cook for 1–2 minutes, or until golden on one side.

Cut the dough into four even portions and shape each into a ball. Press each ball to flatten, then use a lightly floured rolling pin to roll out each ball on a piece of non-stick baking paper to a 25 cm (10 in) round.

Spread the tapenade over the pizzas, then top with the haloumi, charred sides up.

Remove the trays from the oven one at a time to keep them as hot as possible and carefully slide one

pizza (still on the baking paper) onto each tray. Bake for 12 minutes, swapping the trays around after 5 minutes, or until the bases are golden and crisp. Bake the remaining two pizzas.

Meanwhile, rub the lamb with half the pesto. Brush a chargrill pan with olive oil and heat over high heat. Add the lamb and cook for about 1 minute each side for rare, or until cooked to your liking. Transfer the lamb to a chopping board and set aside for 5 minutes to rest. Cut the lamb across the grain into 5 mm (¼ in) slices.

Serve the pizzas immediately, topped with the chargrilled lamb, remaining pesto and parsley leaves, and accompanied by the lemon wedges.

Broccolini chilli pizza

Brocolini florets are smaller than traditional broccoli and the stems are longer and thinner. It is a cross between broccoli and Chinese kale. If you don't have any broccolini you can use 400 g (14 oz) small broccoli florets instead.

Preparation time: 15 minutes
Cooking time: 16 minutes
Makes: two 30 cm (12 in) round pizzas (serves 2–4)

150 g (5½ oz) soft goat's cheese or goat's curd,
  broken into large chunks
70g (2½ oz/⅓ cup) finely grated parmesan cheese or
  Parmigiano Reggiano
80 ml (2½ fl oz/⅓ cup) extra virgin olive oil
3 small red chillies, thinly sliced on the diagonal

4 garlic cloves, thinly sliced
2 bunches broccolini trimmed, halved lengthways
1 quantity pizza dough (see page 168)
12 anchovy fillets, drained on paper towel,
  halved lengthways

Preheat the oven to 220°C (425°F/Gas 7). Place two large, heavy pizza or baking trays in the oven to heat.

Combine the goat's cheese, parmesan cheese and salt and freshly ground black pepper, to taste.

Place the olive oil, chilli and garlic in a small saucepan and cook over low heat for 3 minutes, or until the garlic just turns golden. Remove from the heat and set aside.

Cook the broccolini in a saucepan of boiling water for 1 minute, or until tender-crisp and bright green. Drain and rinse under cold water to refresh. Pat dry with paper towel.

Cut the dough into two even portions and shape each into a ball. Press each ball to flatten, then use a lightly floured rolling pin to roll out each ball on a piece of non-stick baking paper to a 30 cm (12 in) round.

Top the pizzas with the cheese mixture, anchovies and broccolini.

Remove the trays from the oven one at a time to keep them as hot as possible and carefully slide one pizza (still on the baking paper) onto each tray. Bake for 10–12 minutes, swapping the trays around halfway through cooking, or until the bases are golden and crisp.

Serve immediately, drizzled with the chilli and garlic oil and sprinkled with freshly ground black pepper, if desired.

Chorizo pizza rolls

Chorizo is made from roughly chopped pork, with spicy infusions of chilli and smoked paprika (which also gives it its red colouring). There are hundreds of different varieties of chorizo and each will bring a different flavour to this pizza.

Preparation time: 20 minutes (+ plus cooling time)
Cooking time: 40 minutes
Makes: ten rolls (serves 10)

2½ tablespoons olive oil
2 brown onions, halved, thinly sliced
2 chorizo (about 300 g/10½ oz), cut into
  1.5 cm (⅝ in) chunks

1 quantity pizza dough (see page 168)
125 ml (4 fl oz/½ cup) roasted tomato pizza sauce
  (see page 169)
120 g (4¼ oz/1 cup) coarsely grated parmesan cheese

Heat 2 tablespoons of the olive oil in a large frying pan over medium heat. Cook the onion, stirring occasionally, for 10 minutes or until softened. Add the chorizo and cook for a further 10 minutes, stirring occasionally (the onion will start to caramelise so you need to keep it moving so it doesn't burn). Transfer to a plate and set aside to cool.

Preheat the oven to 200°C (400°F/Gas 6). Line two large, heavy baking trays with non-stick baking paper.

Shape the dough into a ball. Press the dough to flatten, then use a lightly floured rolling pin to roll out the dough on a lightly floured surface to a 30 x 45 cm (12 x 17¾ in) rectangle.

With the longest side closest to you, spread the dough evenly with the pizza sauce, leaving a

5 cm (2 in) border at the edge furthest from you and a 1 cm (½ in) border along the remaining three sides. Brush the border with the remaining olive oil. Top the sauce with the cooled onion and chorizo mixture and half the parmesan.

Starting with the edge closest to you, roll up the dough into a log. Cut the log into 10 even portions, wiping the knife clean after each cut. Place five scrolls, cut sides up, on each tray, spacing evenly. Sprinkle the scrolls with the remaining parmesan cheese and then press each to flatten slightly to about 3 cm (1¼ in) thick.

Bake for 20 minutes, swapping the trays around halfway through cooking, or until golden and cooked through. Serve warm.

Pear, prosciutto, blue cheese & walnut pizza

Pears do not ripen well on the tree so they are picked when underripe—store in a cool place for ripening.

Preparation time: 20 minutes
Cooking time: 20 minutes
Makes: two 25 cm (10 in) round pizzas (serves 4 as a starter)

1 tablespoon olive oil, plus extra, for drizzling
2 large, firm, ripe pears (such as Williams)
   (about 700 g/1 lb 9 oz), peeled, cored, thinly sliced
½ quantity pizza dough (see page 168)
65 g (2½ oz/½ cup) coarsely grated mozzarella cheese

75 g (2½ oz) blue cheese, crumbled
60 g (2¼ oz/½ cup) walnut halves, roughly chopped
60 g (2¼ oz) thinly sliced prosciutto, torn into large pieces
60 g (2¼ oz) rocket (arugula)

Heat the olive oil in a large non-stick frying pan over high heat. Add the pears and cook, shaking the pan and flipping them over occasionally, for 5 minutes or until lightly golden.

Preheat the oven to 220°C (425°F/Gas 7). Place two large, heavy pizza or baking trays in the oven to heat.

Cut the dough into two even portions and shape each into a ball. Press each ball to flatten, then use a lightly floured rolling pin to roll out each ball on a piece of non-stick baking paper to a 25 cm (10 in) round.

Sprinkle the pizzas with the mozzarella cheese, then top with the pears.

Remove the trays from the oven one at a time to keep them as hot as possible and carefully slide one pizza (still on the baking paper) onto each tray. Bake for 6 minutes. Remove the pizzas from the oven and top with the blue cheese and walnuts. Return the pizzas to the oven, swapping the trays around, and bake for a further 6–8 minutes or until the bases are golden and crisp.

Top the pizzas with the prosciutto, rocket and some freshly ground black pepper, to taste. Serve immediately, drizzled with a little extra olive oil.

PIZZA DI GAMBERETTI E PESTO

Prawn & pesto pizza

If you don't have time to make the pizza dough, use store-bought mini pizza bases instead. This is the perfect pizza recipe for parties and for entertaining friends.

Preparation time: 30 minutes
Cooking time: 10 minutes
Makes: 24 mini pizzas

2 tablespoons olive oil
1 teaspoon finely chopped basil
1 garlic clove, crushed
24 cooked prawns (shrimp), peeled, deveined

1 quantity pizza dough (see page 168)
60 g (2¼ oz/¼ cup) ready-made pesto
24 small basil leaves
24 pine nuts

Combine the oil, basil, garlic and prawns in a non-metallic bowl. Cover with plastic wrap and refrigerate for 30 minutes.

Preheat the oven to 230°C (450°F/Gas 8). Place two large, heavy pizza or baking trays in the oven to heat.

Cut the dough into 24 even portions and shape each into a ball. Press each ball to flatten, then use a lightly floured rolling pin to roll out each ball on a piece of non-stick baking paper into a circle 3 mm (⅛ in) thick and 4.5 cm (1¾ in) in diameter.

Prick the surfaces with a fork and brush with olive oil.

Spread ½ teaspoon of pesto over each base, leaving a narrow border. Put a prawn, basil leaf and pine nut on each pizza.

Remove the trays from the oven one at a time to keep them as hot as possible and carefully slide 12 mini pizzas (still on the baking paper) onto each tray.

Bake for 8–10 minutes. Serve immediately.

Chapter 3

HEALTHY

*Making your own pizzas allows you to avoid those ingredients which
make takeaway pizzas so unhealthy. The pizza you make at home, using
fresh ingredients, is a healthy and tasty alternative.*

Chargrilled zucchini, mint & ricotta pizza

This pizza is ideal to serve as party fare. Simply cut the pizza into small squares or fingers. To make the reduced-fat pesto, follow the recipe on page 173 but reduce the parmesan cheese to 25 g (1 oz), omit the pine nuts, reduce the olive oil to 1 tablespoon and add 2½ tablespoons of water with the oil.

Preparation time: 10 minutes
Cooking time: 15 minutes
Makes: two 20 x 35 cm (8 x 14 in) rectangle pizzas (serves 4)

1 quantity pizza dough (see page 168)
olive oil spray
2 large zucchini (courgettes), trimmed,
    cut into 5 mm (¼ in) slices on the diagonal
1 quantity reduced-fat mint & chilli pesto (see page 173)

2 teaspoons finely grated lemon zest
165 g (5¾ oz/²/3 cup) firm, fresh low-fat ricotta cheese,
    broken into chunks
small mint leaves, to garnish

Preheat the oven to 230°C (450°F/Gas 8). Place two large, heavy pizza or baking trays in the oven to heat.

Cut the dough into two even portions and shape each into a ball. Press each ball to flatten, then use a lightly floured rolling pin to roll out each ball on a piece of non-stick baking paper to a 20 x 35 cm (8 x 14 in) rectangle.

Heat a chargrill pan over high heat and spray with the olive oil spray. Grill the zucchini for 2–3 minutes each side or until lightly charred

and tender. Spread the pizzas evenly with the pesto, then top with the zucchini, lemon zest and ricotta chunks.

Remove the trays from the oven one at a time to keep them as hot as possible and carefully slide one pizza (still on the baking paper) onto each tray. Bake for 10 minutes, swapping the trays around halfway through cooking, or until the bases are crisp and golden. Serve immediately, sprinkled with the mint.

Seafood pizza with dill, asparagus & lemon

Any combination of seafood can be used for this pizza. It is best to avoid frozen seafood, however, as excess water will prevent the pizza from becoming crisp.

Preparation time: 30 minutes
Cooking time: 24 minutes
Makes: four 25 cm (10 in) round pizzas (serves 4)

1 quantity basic pizza dough (see page 168)
3 tablespoons finely chopped dill,
   plus extra sprigs, to garnish
160 ml (5¼ fl oz/²/₃ cup) roasted tomato
   pizza sauce (see page 169)
105 g (3½ oz/¾ cup) coarsely grated
   low-fat mozzarella cheese
2 bunches asparagus, trimmed, halved
350 g (12 oz) raw prawns (shrimp), peeled,
   deveined, tails left intact

16 scallops, roe removed
250 g (9 oz) squid rings
300 g (10½ oz) skinless firm white fish fillets,
   cut into 2 cm (¾ in) chunks
100g (3¼ oz/¹/₃ cup) low-fat plain yoghurt
1 tablespoon lemon juice
lemon wedges, to serve

Preheat the oven to 230°C (450°F/Gas 8). Place two large, heavy pizza or baking trays in the oven to heat.

Knead 2 tablespoons of the dill into the dough. Cut the dough into four even portions and shape each into a ball. Press each ball to flatten, then use a lightly floured rolling pin to roll out each ball on a piece of non-stick baking paper to a 25 cm (10 in) round. Make a border, pressing with your fingertips 2 cm (¾ in) from the edge.

Spread each pizza with the pizza sauce, then top with the mozzarella cheese and asparagus.

Remove the trays from the oven one at a time to keep them as hot as possible and carefully slide one pizza (still on the baking paper) onto each tray. Bake for 6 minutes. Remove the pizzas from the oven and top with half the prawns, scallops, squid and fish. Return the pizzas to the oven, swapping the trays around, and bake for a further 6 minutes or until the bases are crisp and golden and the seafood is just cooked. Repeat with the remaining two pizzas and seafood.

Meanwhile, combine the yoghurt, lemon juice and the remaining chopped dill. Serve the pizzas immediately, drizzled with a little of the yoghurt mixture, garnished with the dill sprigs and accompanied by the lemon wedges.

Pumpkin & prosciutto pizza with hazelnut salad

To save time, you can use small round pitta breads from the supermarket or frozen mini pizza bases. You can use leftover pumpkin or potato from a roast, and replace the prosciutto with ham.

Preparation time: 10 minutes
Cooking time: 35 minutes
Makes: two 25 cm (10 in) round pizzas (serves 2-4)

2 tablespoons olive oil, plus extra, for greasing
2 garlic cloves, crushed
300 g (10½ oz) butternut pumpkin, (squash) peeled,
    seeded and cut into 1 cm (½ inch) pieces
½ quantity pizza dough (see page 168)
125 ml (4 fl oz/½ cup) tomato pasta sauce
100 g (3½ oz) prosciutto (about 8 thin slices), torn

200 g (7 oz) taleggio or mozzarella cheese,
    cut into 5 mm (¼ inch) slices
2 small handfuls mixed salad leaves
2 small handfuls basil
2 tablespoons hazelnuts, roasted, peeled,
    roughly chopped
2 teaspoons extra virgin olive oil

Preheat the oven to 230°C (450°F/Gas 8). Place two large, heavy pizza or baking trays in the oven to heat.

Combine the olive oil, garlic and pumpkin in a roasting pan and bake for 20 minutes, or until the pumpkin is cooked through and browned lightly. Remove from the pan and set aside.

Cut the dough into two even portions and shape each into a ball. Press each ball to flatten, then use a lightly floured rolling pin to roll out each ball on a piece of non-stick baking paper to a 25 cm (10 in) round. Spread the pasta sauce over each pizza base, then arrange the prosciutto, pumpkin and cheese slices over, leaving a a border of 1 cm (½ in) around the edge of the dough.

Remove the trays from the oven one at a time to keep them as hot as possible and carefully slide one pizza (still on the baking paper) onto each tray.

Bake for 12 minutes, or until the cheese has melted and the pizza is golden brown.

Meanwhile, place the salad leaves and basil in a small bowl, add the nuts and oil, then season to taste with sea salt and freshly ground black pepper. Top the hot pizza with the salad and serve immediately.

Mushroom, ricotta & olive pizza pie

Preparation time: 20 minutes (+ cooling time)
Cooking time: 55 minutes
Makes: one pie (serves 6–8)

4 roma (plum) tomatoes, quartered
½ teaspoon sugar
2 teaspoons olive oil
2 garlic cloves, crushed
1 brown onion, thinly sliced

750 g (1 lb 10 oz) mushroom caps, trimmed, sliced
1 quantity pizza dough (see page 168)
250 g (9 oz) firm, fresh low-fat ricotta cheese
2 tablespoons sliced black olives
1 small handful basil leaves, to serve

Preheat the oven to 210°C (415°F/Gas 6–7). Line a baking tray with non-stick baking paper.

Place the tomato quarters on the lined tray, sprinkle with the sugar, and season with salt and freshly ground black pepper. Roast the tomato for 20 minutes, or until the edges start to darken.

Meanwhile, heat the oil in a large frying pan over medium heat and cook the garlic and onion for 8 minutes, or until soft. Increase the heat to medium–high, add half the mushrooms and cook, stirring occasionally, until they are tender and all the liquid has evaporated. Transfer to a bowl. Repeat with the remaining mushrooms. Set aside to cool.

Shape the dough into a ball and press to flatten. Use a lightly floured rolling pin to roll out the dough on a 40 cm (16 in) square piece of non-stick baking paper to a 38 cm (15 in) round.

Slide the pizza (still on the baking paper) onto a large, heavy baking tray. Spread with the ricotta, leaving a 5 cm (2 in) border. Top with the mushrooms, tomatoes and olives. Fold the dough edge over the filling to form a border

Bake for 25 minutes, or until the pizza crust is golden and cooked through. Serve immediately, sprinkled with the basil.

Spinach, grape & rosemary pizza with cornmeal crust

Cornmeal is made from ground corn, usually without the corn skin or germ and has a coarse texture. Cornmeal doesn't contain gluten so it is generally used to make quick breads or breads with a cake-like texture.

Preparation time: 15 minutes
Cooking time: 20 minutes
Makes: four 16 x 25 cm (6¼ x 10 in) rectangle pizzas (serves 4)

1 quantity pizza dough (see page 168), made using 100 g (3½ oz) cornmeal instead of 100 g (3½ oz/⅔ cup) of the plain (all-purpose) flour
125 g (4½ oz/½ cup) light sour cream
120 g (4¼ oz) firm, fresh low-fat ricotta cheese
2 tablespoons chopped rosemary

100 g (3½ oz) baby English spinach leaves
300 g (10½ oz) small, seedless black grapes
50 g (1¾ oz/⅓ cup) pine nuts
2 teaspoons extra virgin olive oil
2 teaspoons white wine vinegar

Preheat the oven to 230°C (450°F/Gas 8). Place two large, heavy baking trays in the oven to heat.

Cut the dough into four even portions and shape each into a ball. Press each ball to flatten, then use a lightly floured rolling pin to roll out each ball on a piece of non-stick baking paper to a 16 x 25 cm (6¼ x 10 in) rectangle. Make a border, pressing with your fingertips 2 cm (¾ in) from the edge.

Combine the sour cream, ricotta, rosemary and salt and freshly ground black pepper, to taste. Spread the sour cream mixture over the pizzas, leaving a small border around the edge, then top with the spinach and grapes.

Remove the trays from the oven one at a time to keep them as hot as possible and carefully slide one pizza (still on the baking paper) onto each tray. Bake for 5 minutes. Remove the pizzas from the oven and sprinkle with half the pine nuts. Return the pizzas to the oven, swapping the trays around, and bake for a further 5 minutes or until the bases are crisp and golden. Repeat with the remaining two pizzas and pine nuts.

Serve the pizzas immediately, brushed with the combined oil and vinegar and sprinkled with freshly ground black pepper, if desired.

Food Journey

TOMATOES

∞∞∞∞∞∞∞∞∞∞∞∞∞∞∞∞∞∞∞∞∞∞∞∞∞∞∞∞∞∞

When the Spanish initially brought the tomato back to Europe, it was mostly used as a decorative plant. The Neapolitans were the first Europeans to embrace this new fruit, growing them from seeds brought from the New World, and it was in Naples that the tomato transformed the pizza.

Although botanically a fruit, the tomato, another gift of inestimable value to the world's cuisines—especially Italian—from South America, is used mainly as a vegetable. So thoroughly has the tomato been assimilated that it's difficult to imagine life in the Western world (no tomato sauce or pizza!) before it arrived in Naples in the sixteenth century. First, people thought of it as a medicinal plant, and it took a generation before it began to appear on the table. Today, tomatoes are grown worldwide, America and Italy being the largest producers for canning, sauces, pastes and purées. There are more than 1,000 varieties, in numerous sizes, shapes and colours. Most varieties are red, although others are yellow or pink. Unripe green tomatoes are used in pickles and chutneys.

The best flavoured are those that are vine-ripened. Tomatoes should be firm and brightly coloured, with no wrinkles and a strong tomato smell, and should be eaten immediately. Buy only in small quantities (unless making sauce), or buy some greener than others. For salads and pasta sauces, buy only the reddest, ripest tomatoes. Remember, uniformity of shape or colour has no relation to flavour, only to marketing.

There are several main types of tomatoes:

Cherry tomatoes: Come in various sizes but essentially are a tiny variety of tomato. Some are red, others are yellow and some are pear shaped. Good for salads or used whole or halved in stews and pasta sauces.

Roma (plum) tomatoes: Commercially used for canning and drying. They have few seeds and a dry flesh which makes them ideal in sauces or purées.

Beef steak tomatoes: These are larger tomatoes, either smooth and rounded or more irregular with ridges. Can be used for stuffing or in salads.

Round tomatoes: The most common tomato commercially bred to be round and red. Can be bought vine-ripened, on the vine or in different varieties liked the striped tigerella, yellow or orange coloured. An all-purpose tomato.

Pumpkin & ricotta pizza

Sage leaves were traditionally used in Italian cuisine to flavour butter served with pasta. Use sparingly as the flavour can be strong.

Preparation time: 20 minutes
Cooking time: 40 minutes
Makes: four 23 cm (9 in) square pizzas (serves 4)

700 g (1 lb 9 oz) butternut pumpkin (squash),
   halved lengthways, cut into 5 mm (¼ in) slices
1 garlic bulb, divided into cloves, unpeeled
2 tablespoons olive oil
1 quantity pizza dough (see page 168)

230 g (8 oz/1 cup) firm, fresh low-fat ricotta cheese,
   broken into large chunks
140 g (5 oz/1 cup) frozen peas
1 handful small sage leaves, to serve

Preheat the oven to 200°C (400°F/Gas 6). Place the pumpkin, garlic cloves and olive oil in a bowl and toss to combine. Spread evenly on a baking tray and roast for 20 minutes, or until the pumpkin and garlic are soft. Allow to cool slightly. When cool enough to handle, remove the skins from the garlic cloves.

Meanwhile, increase oven temperature to 230°C (450°F/Gas 8). Place two large, heavy baking trays in the oven to heat.

Cut the dough into four even portions and shape each into a ball. Press each ball to flatten, then use a lightly floured rolling pin to roll out each ball on a piece of non-stick baking paper to a 23 cm (9 in) square. Make a border, pressing with your fingertips 2 cm (¾ in) from the edge.

Top the pizzas with the ricotta chunks, peas, pumpkin, garlic and salt and freshly ground black pepper, to taste.

Remove the trays from the oven one at a time to keep them as hot as possible and carefully slide one pizza (still on the baking paper) onto each tray. Bake for 10 minutes, swapping the trays around halfway through cooking, or until the bases are golden. Bake the remaining two pizzas. Serve the pizzas immediately, sprinkled with the

PIZZA CON FUNGHI, SPINACI, ORIGANO E CAPRINO

Mushroom, spinach, oregano & goat's curd pizza

The goat's curd can be replaced if necessary with low-fat ricotta or soft goat's cheese.
Any combination of mushrooms can be used, such as shiitake, button or enoki.

Preparation time: 20 minutes
Cooking time: 26 minutes
Makes: four 25 cm (10 in) round pizzas (serves 4)

olive oil spray
200 g (7 oz) Swiss brown mushrooms, sliced
150 g (5½ oz) oyster mushrooms, sliced
2 garlic cloves, crushed

250 g (9 oz) baby English spinach leaves
1 quantity wholemeal pizza dough (see page 168)
2 tablespoons chopped oregano
120 g (4¼ oz) goat's curd, broken into chunks

Preheat the oven to 230°C (450°F/Gas 8). Place two large, heavy pizza or baking trays in the oven to heat.

Heat a large non-stick frying pan over high heat and spray with the olive oil spray. Add the mushrooms and cook, stirring, for 3–4 minutes or until golden. Add the garlic and spinach and cook for another 2 minutes, or until the spinach is just wilted.

Cut the dough into four even portions and shape each into a ball. Press each ball to flatten, then use a lightly floured rolling pin to roll out each ball on

a piece of non-stick baking paper to a 25 cm (10 in) round. Make a border, pressing with your fingertips 2 cm (¾ in) from the edge.

Spread the mushroom mixture evenly over the pizzas, then top with the oregano and goat's curd.

Remove the trays from the oven one at a time to keep them as hot as possible and carefully slide one pizza (still on the baking paper) onto each tray. Bake for 10 minutes, swapping the trays around halfway through cooking, or until the bases are crisp and golden. Bake the remaining two pizzas. Serve immediately.

Moroccan chicken pizza

Preserved lemon is available from the condiments section of larger supermarkets and delicatessens. If you can't find it, you can replace it with the zest of half a lemon, white pith removed and very thinly sliced.

Preparation time: 25 minutes
Cooking time: 30 minutes
Makes: four 24 cm (9½ in) round pizzas (serves 4)

1 teaspoon ground cumin
1 teaspoon ground coriander
½ teaspoon ground cinnamon
400 g (14 oz) boneless, skinless chicken breasts, thinly sliced
olive oil spray
1 large red onion, thinly sliced
200 g (7 oz) baby English spinach leaves

1 tablespoon currants
1 quantity pizza dough (see page 168)
160 ml (5¼ fl oz/²/₃ cup) pizza sauce (see page 169)
90 g (3¼ oz/²/₃ cup) coarsely grated low-fat mozzarella cheese
1 handful flat-leaf (Italian) parsley leaves
½ preserved lemon, or to taste, flesh and white pith removed, thinly sliced

Combine the cumin, coriander and cinnamon in a mixing bowl. Toss the chicken in the spice mixture to coat evenly.

Heat a large non-stick frying pan over high heat and spray with the olive oil spray. Cook the onion, stirring occasionally, for 3–4 minutes or until golden. Add the chicken and cook, stirring occasionally, for another 3–4 minutes or until lightly golden. Add the spinach and currants, and cook for a further 1 minute, or until the spinach is just wilted. Remove from the heat.

Preheat the oven to 230°C (450°F/Gas 8). Place two large, heavy pizza or baking trays in the oven to heat.

Cut the dough into four even portions and shape each into a ball. Press each ball to flatten, then use a lightly floured rolling pin to roll out each ball on a piece of non-stick baking paper to a 24 cm (9½ in) round. Make a border, pressing with your fingertips 2 cm (¾ in) from the edge.

Spread the pizzas evenly with the pizza sauce, then top with the chicken and spinach mixture. Sprinkle with the mozzarella cheese.

Remove the trays from the oven one at a time to keep them as hot as possible and carefully slide one pizza (still on the baking paper) onto each tray. Bake for 10 minutes, swapping the trays around halfway through cooking, or until the bases are golden and crisp. Bake the remaining two pizzas.

Meanwhile, combine the parsley and preserved lemon. Serve the pizzas immediately, topped with the parsley salad.

Tomato, chicken & broccoli pizza

For extra flavour, sprinkle the pizzas with dried red chilli flakes or dried oregano before baking.

Preparation time: 20 minutes
Cooking time: 22 minutes
Makes: four 25 cm (10 in) round pizzas (serves 4)

350 g (12 oz) broccoli, trimmed, cut into small florets
1 quantity pizza dough (see page 168)
90 g (3¼ oz/⅓ cup) tomato paste (concentrated purée)
300 g (10½ oz/2 cups) cooked boneless, skinless, chicken breast, roughly shredded

250 g (9 oz) mixed cherry tomatoes, halved
200 g (7 oz) bocconcini (fresh baby mozzarella cheese), torn into chunks
basil leaves, shredded, to garnish

Preheat the oven to 230°C (450°F/Gas 8). Place two large, heavy pizza or baking trays in the oven to heat.

Cook the broccoli in a large saucepan of lightly salted boiling water for 1–2 minutes, or until bright green and just tender. Refresh under cold running water, then drain well.

Cut the dough into four even portions and shape each into a ball. Press each ball to flatten, then use a lightly floured rolling pin to roll out each ball on a piece of non-stick baking paper to a 25 cm (10 in) round.

Spread the bases evenly with the tomato paste. Top with the shredded chicken, tomato halves, broccoli and bocconcini.

Remove the trays from the oven one at a time to keep them as hot as possible and carefully slide one pizza (still on the baking paper) onto each tray. Bake for 10 minutes, swapping the trays around halfway through cooking, or until the bases are crisp and golden. Bake the remaining two pizzas. Serve the pizzas immediately, sprinkled with the basil.

Small pizzas

Preparation time: 5 minutes
Cooking time: 10 minutes
Makes: 10 small pizzas

1 quantity pizza dough (see page 168)
cornmeal, for dusting
250 g (9 oz) mozzarella cheese
1 tablespoon olive oil

GARLIC & ROSEMARY PIZZETTE
4 garlic cloves, crushed
2 teaspoons chopped rosemary
1½ tablespoons olive oil
50 g (1¾ oz) grated parmesan cheese
3 garlic cloves, thinly sliced

TOMATO & OLIVE PIZZETTE
200 g (7 oz) pitted black olives, diced
400 g (14 oz) roma (plum) tomatoes, diced
3 garlic cloves, crushed
2 tablespoons finely shredded basil
60 ml (2 fl oz/¼ cup) tablespoons olive oil
5 small basil sprigs

Preheat the oven to 240°C (475°F/Gas 9). Form the pizza dough into 10 bases. Dust two baking trays with cornmeal and place the pizza bases on the trays. Grate the mozzarella cheese. Brush the pizza bases with the oil, then sprinkle with mozzarella cheese. Make five garlic and rosemary pizzette and five tomato and olive pizzette.

To make the garlic and rosemary pizzette, scatter five bases with the crushed garlic and rosemary and drizzle with the oil. Sprinkle with parmesan cheese and garnish with some slices of garlic.

To make the tomato and olive pizzette, mix together the olives, tomato, garlic and shredded basil, and spoon over the remaining bases. Drizzle with the oil and garnish with the basil sprigs.

Bake the pizzette for 10 minutes, or until the bases are crisp and golden.

Chapter 4

CHEATS

❊❊❊❊❊❊❊❊❊❊❊❊❊❊❊❊❊❊❊❊❊❊❊❊❊❊❊❊❊❊❊❊❊❊❊❊❊❊

There is no need to miss out on a pizza when you don't have the time to prepare fresh dough for the base. These recipes use simple store-cupboard alternatives and still deliver a delicious pizza experience.

Eggplant, semi-dried tomato & olive pizza

Sun-drying was originally an Italian method for preserving tomatoes. The basic method is to cut them in half, sprinkle with salt and leave in the sun. The salt dehydrates the tomato and concentrates the falvour. Semi-dried tomatoes are partially dried in a dehydrator and immersed in oil to preserve for any length of time.

Preparation time: 10 minutes
Cooking time: 10–12 minutes
Makes: two 20 x 29 cm (8 x 11½ in) rectangle pizzas (serves 4)

two 20 x 29 cm (8 x 11½ in) ready-made rectangle
  pizza bases
125 ml (4 fl oz/½ cup) tomato passata (puréed tomatoes)
100 g (3½ oz) thinly sliced hot salami
200 g (7 oz) chargrilled sliced eggplant (aubergine)
200 g (7 oz) bocconcini (fresh baby mozzarella cheese),
  torn into chunks

100 g (3½ oz/½ cup) semi-dried (sun-blushed)
  tomatoes, sliced
75 g (2¾ oz/½ cup) pitted kalamata olives
small basil leaves, to garnish

Preheat the oven to 220°C (425°F/Gas 7). Place two large, heavy baking trays in the oven to heat.

Spread each pizza base evenly with the tomato passata. Top with the salami, eggplant, bocconcini, tomato and olives.

Remove the trays from the oven one at a time to keep them as hot as possible and carefully place one pizza on each tray. Bake for 10–12 minutes, swapping the trays around halfway through cooking, or until the bases are crisp and golden.

Serve immediately, sprinkled with the basil.

Spicy smoked chicken, tomato & spinach pizza

You can use small pitta breads instead of the naan bread.

Preparation time: 15 minutes
Cooking time: 10 minutes
Makes: four oval pizzas (serves 4)

80 ml (2½ fl oz/⅓ cup) tomato passata
  (puréed tomatoes)
¼ teaspoon dried red chilli flakes
four x 70 g (2½ oz) naan bread
200 g (7 oz) smoked chicken breast fillet, thinly sliced
125 g (4½ oz) marinated artichoke hearts, drained,
  halved lengthways

2 roma (plum) tomatoes, seeded, diced
1 small red onion, thinly sliced
125 g (4½ oz/1 cup) coarsely grated
  mozzarella cheese
40 g (1½ oz) baby English spinach leaves, to garnish

Preheat the oven to 230°C (450°F/Gas 8). Place two large, heavy baking trays in the oven to heat.

Combine the tomato passata and chilli flakes in a bowl. Spread the naan breads evenly with the passata. Top with the chicken, artichokes, tomato, onion and mozzarella cheese.

Remove the trays from the oven one at a time to keep them as hot as possible and carefully place two pizzas onto each tray. Bake for 10 minutes, swapping the trays around halfway through cooking, or until the bases are golden. Serve immediately, topped with the spinach.

Tuna, tomato & chilli pizza

Preparation time: 10 minutes
Cooking time: 20 minutes
Makes: four 24 cm (9½ in) round pizzas (serves 4)

four 24 cm (9½ in) thin round pizza bases
160 ml (5¼ fl oz/²/₃ cup) tomato passata
  (puréed tomatoes) or ready-made pizza sauce
220 g (7¾ oz) fresh buffalo mozzarella cheese,
  thinly sliced
2 garlic cloves, thinly sliced

425 g (15 oz) tinned tuna in oil
2 small vine-ripened tomatoes, roughly chopped
2 teaspoons dried red chilli flakes
2 tablespoons roughly chopped flat-leaf (Italian)
  parsley, to garnish

Preheat the oven to 200°C (400°F/Gas 6).

Place each pizza on a piece of non-stick baking paper. Spread the pizzas evenly with the tomato passata, then top with the mozzarella cheese and garlic.

Drain the tuna in a sieve over a bowl to catch the oil. Break the tuna into large chunks and scatter over the pizzas with the tomato. Sprinkle with the

chilli and drizzle each evenly with the reserved tuna oil. Season with salt.

Carefully slide two of the pizzas onto two large, heavy pizza or baking trays. Bake for 10 minutes, swapping the trays around halfway through cooking, or until golden. Bake the remaining two pizzas. Serve immediately, sprinkled with the parsley.

Chicken, vegetable & pesto pizza

Preparation time: 10 minutes
Cooking time: 15 minutes
Makes: two 20 x 30 cm (8 x 12 in) rectangle pizzas (serves 4)

two 20 x 30 cm (8 x 12 in) ready-made thick rectangle
  pizza bases
125 ml (4 fl oz/½ cup) tomato passata (puréed
  tomatoes) or ready-made pizza sauce
125 g (4½ oz/1 cup) coarsely grated mozzarella cheese
150 g (5½ oz) barbecue chicken meat,
  coarsely shredded

280 g (10 oz) jar mixed chargrilled vegetables
  in oil, drained
100 g (3½ oz/⅔ cup) crumbled feta cheese
2 tablespoons ready-made pesto

Preheat the oven to 200°C (400°F/Gas 6). Place two large, heavy baking trays in the oven to heat.

Place each pizza on a piece of non-stick baking paper. Spread the pizzas evenly with the tomato passata, top with the mozzarella cheese, chicken, chargrilled vegetables and feta, and then dollop the pesto over.

Remove the trays from the oven one at a time to keep them as hot as possible and carefully slide one pizza (still on the baking paper) onto each tray. Bake for 15 minutes, swapping the trays around halfway through cooking, or until the bases are crisp and golden. Serve immediately.

Artichoke, olive & thyme pizza

Pitta bread is a flatbread typical of the bread baked in Lebanon. It is available in most supermarkets as well as speciality stores. Each bread (called a loaf) is about the size of a dinner plate. They are thin so make a great crispy pizza base.

Preparation time: 15 minutes
Cooking time: 16 minutes
Makes: four large round pizzas (serves 4)

4 large round pitta breads
280 g (10 oz) jar marinated artichoke hearts, drained
160 ml (5¼ fl oz/²/₃ cup) tomato passata (puréed tomatoes) or ready-made pizza sauce
105 g (3½ oz/¾ cup) coarsely grated mozzarella cheese
110 g (3¾ oz/²/₃ cup) pitted kalamata olives, halved
120 g (4¼ oz) goat's cheese, thickly sliced
2 tablespoons thyme leaves

Preheat the oven to 200°C (400°F/Gas 6).

Place each pitta bread on a piece of non-stick baking paper. Cut the artichoke hearts into 2 cm (¾ in) wedges. Spread the breads evenly with the tomato passata, then top with half the mozzarella cheese, the artichokes, olives, goat's cheese and thyme. Top with the remaining mozzarella cheese. Season with salt.

Carefully slide two pizzas onto two separate large, heavy pizza or baking trays. Bake for 8 minutes, swapping the trays around halfway through cooking, or until the bases are crisp and golden. Bake the remaining two pizzas. Serve immediately.

Hot & fiery white bean, salami & ricotta pizza

If you want less 'heat' in your pizzas, substitute mild salami for the hot Spanish-style salami or reduce the quantity of chilli flakes.

Preparation time: 10 minutes
Cooking time: 20 minutes
Makes: four 30 cm (12 in) round pizzas (serves 4–8)

four 30 cm (12 in) ready-made thick, round pizza bases
   with tomato sauce
230 g (8 oz/1 cup) firm, fresh ricotta cheese
2 teaspoons dried red chilli flakes, or to taste

400 g (14 oz) tinned cannellini beans, rinsed, drained
225 g (8 oz) hot Spanish-style salami, thinly sliced
200 g (7 oz/2 cups) coarsely grated gruyère cheese
1 handful oregano leaves

Preheat the oven to 220°C (425°F/Gas 7). Place two large, heavy pizza or baking trays in the oven to heat.

Place each pizza base on a piece of non-stick baking paper. Spread the pizzas with the ricotta and sprinkle with the chilli flakes, then top with the cannellini beans, salami and gruyère, and sprinkle with half the oregano.

Remove the trays from the oven one at a time to keep them as hot as possible and carefully slide one pizza (still on the baking paper) onto each tray. Bake for 10 minutes, swapping the trays halfway through cooking, or until the bases are crisp and golden. Bake the remaining two pizzas.

Serve immediately, sprinkled with the remaining oregano leaves.

PIZZA CON SALSICCIA E POMODORI SECCHI
Sausage & semi-dried tomato pizza

Preparation time: 10 minutes
Cooking time: 12 minutes
Makes: four 15 x 21 cm (6 x 8¼ in) rectangle pizzas (serves 4)

two 21 x 30 cm (8¼ x 12 in) ready-made rectangle
  garlic-and-herb pizza bases, halved crossways
160 ml (5¼ fl oz/²⁄₃ cup) tomato passata (puréed
  tomatoes)
260 g (9¼ oz) coarsely grated mozzarella cheese
105 g (3½ oz/½ cup) semi-dried (sun-blushed)
  tomatoes

90 g (3¼ oz) chargrilled capsicum (pepper), sliced
4 thin pork sausages (about 350 g/12 oz), skins
  removed, filling crumbled
60 g (2¼ oz) baby rocket (arugula)

Preheat the oven to 220°C (425°F/Gas 7). Place
two large, heavy baking trays in the oven to heat.

Place each pizza on a piece of non-stick baking
paper. Spread the pizzas evenly with the tomato
passata, leaving a small border, then top with the
mozzarella cheese, tomatoes, capsicum and
crumbled sausage.

Remove the trays from the oven one at a time to
keep them as hot as possible and carefully slide

two pizzas (still on the baking paper) onto each
tray. Bake for 12 minutes, swapping the trays
around halfway through cooking, or until golden
and the sausage is cooked.

Serve the pizzas immediately, topped with the
rocket and seasoned with freshly ground
black pepper.

Ham, olive & artichoke pizza

You can use oregano leaves instead of the parsley.

Preparation time: 10 minutes
Cooking time: 15 minutes
Makes: six small round pizzas (serves 6 as a starter)

6 pitta breads
200 g (7 oz) coarsely grated edam cheese
240 g (8½ oz) shaved leg ham
100 g (3½ oz) stuffed green olives, halved

6 marinated artichoke hearts, drained, sliced crossways
  into thirds
1 small handful flat-leaf (Italian) parsley leaves

Preheat the oven to 220°C (425°F/Gas 7). Place two large, heavy baking trays in the oven to heat.

Top the pitta breads with two-thirds of the edam, cheese then the ham, olives and artichokes. Sprinkle with the remaining edam.

Remove the trays from the oven one at a time to keep them as hot as possible and carefully place three pizzas on each tray. Bake for 15 minutes, swapping the trays halfway through cooking, or until the bases are crisp and golden.

Serve the pizzas immediately, sprinkled with the parsley leaves.

Smoked salmon pizzas

Dill is a great garnish for fish and seafood. Its feathery leaves have a strong aniseed flavour. For this recipe, cut small sprigs and add to the pizza after cooking.

Preparation time: 15 minutes
Cooking time: 15 minutes
Makes: six small oval pizzas (serves 6)

6 small oval pitta breads
230 g (8 oz/1 cup) firm, fresh low-fat ricotta cheese
1 small red onion, thinly sliced
1 tablespoon baby capers, rinsed, drained

125 g (4½ oz) smoked salmon slices
dill sprigs, to garnish
lemon wedges, to serve

Preheat the oven to 180°C (350°F/Gas 4). Line two baking trays with non-stick baking paper.

Place the pitta breads on the trays. Place the ricotta in a bowl, season with salt and freshly ground black pepper and stir to combine. Spread the ricotta over the pitta breads, leaving a small border around the edges. Top with the onion and capers.

Bake the pizzas for 15 minutes, swapping the trays around halfway through cooking, or until the bases are crisp around the edges.

Top with the smoked salmon and dill. Season with freshly ground black pepper, to taste, if desired. Accompany with the lemon wedges. Serve immediately.

Pizzette

Keep packets of store-bought mini pizza bases in your freezer for a quick and tasty meal.

Preparation time: 5 minutes
Cooking time: 15 minutes
Makes: four mini pizzas

4 ready-made mini pizza bases
2 tablespoons tomato paste (concentrated purée)
1 garlic clove, crushed
1 teaspoon dried oregano

20 g (¾ oz) lean shaved ham
1 small handful of rocket (arugula) leaves
2 teaspoons grated light mozzarella cheese
extra virgin olive oil for drizzling

Preheat the oven to 200°C (400°F/ Gas 6). Place pizza bases on a baking tray.

Combine the tomato paste, garlic, oregano and 1 tablespoon of water. Spread the tomato paste mixture over each base then top with the ham, rocket and mozzarella cheese.

Bake for 12-15 minutes, or until crisp and golden on the edges. Just before serving, drizzle with extra virgin olive oil.

Goat's cheese pizza with artichokes and olives

This recipe uses tomato pasta sauce rather than tomato pizza sauce. However, you can use either.

Preparation time: 10 minutes
Cooking time: 20 minutes
Makes: one 25 cm (10 in) round pizza (serves 2)

80 ml (2½ fl oz/⅓ cup) Italian tomato pasta sauce
150 g (5½ oz) marinated artichokes, quartered
70 g (2½ oz/¼ cup) pitted Kalamata olives
1 garlic clove, thinly sliced

50 g (1¾ oz) goat's cheese, crumbled
olive oil, for drizzling
1 handful fresh oregano, chopped, to garnish

Preheat the oven to 220°C (425°F/Gas 7). Place one large, heavy baking tray in the oven to heat.

Top the pizza base with two-thirds of the tomato pasta sauce. Evenly scatter the artichoke quarters, olives and the garlic over the pasta sauce, then top with the crumbled goat's cheese.

Lightly drizzle the surface of the pizza with olive oil.

Remove the tray from the oven and carefully place the pizza on the tray. Bake for 20 minutes, or until the base is crisp and golden.

Sprinkle with fresh oregano and season with salt and freshly ground black pepper.

Chapter 5

VEGETARIAN

∞∞∞∞∞∞∞∞∞∞∞∞∞∞∞∞∞∞∞∞∞∞∞∞∞∞∞∞∞∞∞

*You don't have to be a vegetarian to love these pizzas, topped
with a fantastic range of cheeses, vegetables and herbs.
Pizzas aren't just for meat lovers!*

Leek, blue cheese & rosemary pizza

Cook the leeks until they are tender and sweet. If undercooked, they will be too crunchy and, if overcooked, leeks will turn slimy. Leeks often contain dirt between their layers and need to be washed thoroughly.

Preparation time: 20 minutes
Cooking time: 40 minutes
Makes: four 24 cm (9½ in) round pizzas (serves 4)

3 large leeks (about 1.5 kg/3 lb 6 oz), white part
   only, trimmed, washed well
60 ml (2 fl oz/¼ cup) olive oil
2 rosemary sprigs

1 quantity pizza dough (see page 168)
200 g (7 oz) firm blue cheese, roughly crumbled
50 g (1¾ oz/⅓ cup) pine nuts

Cut the leeks into 1 cm (½ in) thick rounds. Heat the olive oil in a large saucepan over medium heat. Add the leeks and 1 rosemary sprig, cover and cook, stirring occasionally, for 15 minutes or until the leeks are tender. Discard the rosemary sprig. Transfer the leeks to a colander and drain well, pressing down on the leeks gently to expel as much liquid as possible. Cool slightly.

Preheat the oven to 220°C (425°F/Gas 7). Place two large, heavy pizza or baking trays in the oven to heat.

Cut the dough into four even portions and shape each into a ball. Press each ball to flatten, then use a lightly floured rolling pin to roll out each ball on a piece of non-stick baking paper to a 24 cm (9½ in) round.

Spread the bases evenly with the leeks, then top with the blue cheese.

Remove the trays from the oven one at a time to keep them as hot as possible and carefully slide one pizza (still on the baking paper) onto each tray. Bake for 7 minutes. Remove the pizzas from the oven and sprinkle them with half the pine nuts. Return the pizzas to the oven, swapping the trays around, and bake for a further 5 minutes or until the pizza bases are crisp and golden, and the cheese is bubbling. Repeat with the remaining two pizzas and pine nuts.

Serve immediately, sprinkled with the leaves from the remaining rosemary sprig.

PIZZA CON CECI E ZUCCA

Chickpea & pumpkin pizza

Unlike many canned vegetables, which lose much of their nutritional value, the canning process does not harm many of the key nutrients found in chickpeas. To drain, place them in a strainer and rinse thoroughly.

Preparation time: 25 minutes
Cooking time: 35 minutes
Makes: six 16 cm (6¼ in) round pizzas (serves 6 as a starter or snack)

500 g (1 lb 2 oz) butternut pumpkin (squash), peeled, seeded
60 ml (2 fl oz/¼ cup) olive oil
400 g (14 oz) tinned chickpeas, rinsed, drained
1 quantity pizza sauce (see page 169)
1 tablespoon chopped sage leaves
1 quantity pizza dough (see page 168)
250 g (9 oz) coarsely grated Swiss cheese
24 sage leaves

Preheat the oven to 180°C (350°F/Gas 4). Cut the pumpkin into wedges about 4 cm (1½ in) thick, then cut widthways into slices about 8 mm (⅜ in) thick. Place in a large roasting dish, drizzle with the olive oil and roast for 15 minutes or until tender. Set aside.

Increase the oven temperature to 220°C (425°F/Gas 7). Place three large, heavy pizza or baking trays in the oven to heat.

Place the chickpeas in a bowl and use a fork to crush roughly. Add the pizza sauce and the chopped sage and stir to combine.

Cut the dough into six even portions and shape each into a ball. Press each ball to flatten, then use a lightly floured rolling pin to roll out each ball on a piece of non-stick baking paper to a 16 cm (6¼ in) round.

Spread the pizzas evenly with the chickpea mixture, then sprinkle with the cheese. Top with the roasted pumpkin and the sage leaves.

Remove the trays from the oven one at a time to keep them as hot as possible and carefully slide two pizzas (still on the baking paper) onto each tray. Bake for 15–20 minutes, swapping the trays around halfway through cooking, or until the bases are crisp and golden, and the cheese is bubbling. Serve immediately.

CHEESE

◇◇◇◇◇◇◇◇◇◇◇◇◇◇◇◇◇◇◇◇◇◇◇◇◇◇◇◇◇◇◇

As well as making famous cheeses such as Parmigiano Reggiano and mozzarella cheese, Italian cheesemakers create hundreds of regional cheeses, fresh and aged, and many are rarely found outside Italy.

The history of cheese in Italy is very closely related to the country's varied geography. The rich mountainous pastures of the North produce hundreds of cheeses such as fontina, Gorgonzola, mascarpone, Asiago, Grana Padano and Taleggio. In the Centre, Emilia-Romagna is the home of Parmigiano Reggiano (parmesan cheese), perhaps Italy's most famous cheese. Tuscany and Umbria produce fresh pecorinos, while the sparser and hotter South is more suited to farming sheep and goats than cows. The sheep's and goat's cheeses of this region are usually harder than the French chèvre and are suitable for grating, though you can also find soft, fresh cheeses like sheep's ricotta. The South is also the home of *pasta filata*, cheeses made from stretched-out curds like mozzarella cheese and provolone. In Campania, buffalo milk is used to make mozzarella cheese.

Many of the traditional methods for making cheese are safeguarded by *consorzi* (cooperatives), who have imposed their own rules for production to ensure their cheeses are made to the highest quality, using the best milk in each area. The rules for production can include methods passed down through centuries, such as milking parmesan cheese cows by hand, and this explains their often higher cost. Cheeses from *consorzi* are usually awarded a DOC (*Denominazione di Origine Controllata*) rating in the form of a brand or stamp on the rind.

Italian cheeses can be made from cow's, buffalo's, goat's and sheep's milk. Cow's milk is used more in the North, while buffaloes are farmed around Naples and almost all of the milk is used to make mozzarella cheese *di bufala*. Goat's and sheep's cheeses are becoming increasingly popular. Most are produced in Tuscany, Umbria and the South. Both pasteurised and unpasteurised cheeses are made in Italy, with unpasteurised or partly unpasteurised cheeses, such as *caciocavallo* and provolone, continuing to develop as they age.

Italian cheeses are also divided into hard and soft cheeses. Hard cheeses have a water content of less than 40 per cent and include those cheeses used for cooking such as Grana Padano and pecorino. Soft cheeses have a water content of more than 40 per cent and are best eaten as soon as possible after being made. They include cheeses such as mascarpone and mozzarella cheese, which should be eaten the day they are made.

Unlike French cheeses, Italian cheeses are more famous for their use in cooking than for being eaten as a separate cheese course. In Italy though, cheeses are often eaten at every course, in cooking and as table cheeses. Cooking cheeses are known as *formaggio per cucina* and perhaps the most famous is Parmigiano Reggiano, rarely eaten as part of a cheese platter outside of Italy. Table cheeses are known as *formaggio da tavola*. Both fresh and hard cheeses are eaten on their own.

Taleggio
Cademartori
£ 2500 hg

LUMACHUN DI LENTICCHIE

Lentil lamachun

Although you can use any variety of tomato in this recipe, the roma (plum) tomato has fewer seeds and a dry flesh that makes it ideal for this pizza.

Preparation time: 20 minutes
Cooking time: 26 minutes
Makes: six pizzas (serves 6)

500 g (1 lb 2 oz) ripe roma (plum) tomatoes
2½ tablespoons olive oil, plus extra, for greasing
1 brown onion, finely chopped
2 garlic cloves, crushed
1½ tablespoons tomato paste (concentrated purée)
1 teaspoon sweet paprika
1 teaspoon ground allspice

¼ teaspoon cayenne pepper, or to taste (optional)
800 g (1 lb 12 oz) tinned brown lentils, rinsed, drained
1 bunch coriander (cilantro), chopped, plus extra sprigs, to garnish
1 quantity wholemeal pizza dough (see page 168)
125 g (4½ oz) feta cheese, roughly crumbled

Preheat the oven to 220°C (425°F/Gas 7). Lightly grease two large, heavy baking trays with olive oil.

Cut the tomatoes into quarters lengthways and remove the seeds. Chop the tomatoes into 5 mm (¼ in) pieces.

Heat the olive oil in a large heavy-based saucepan over medium heat. Cook the onion and garlic, stirring often, for 3–4 minutes or until starting to soften. Add the tomato paste and spices then cook, stirring constantly, for 1–2 minutes or until fragrant. Stir in the tomato and lentils then remove from the heat and cool slightly. Stir in the coriander.

Cut the dough into six even portions and shape each into a ball. Press each ball to flatten, then use a lightly floured rolling pin to roll out each ball on a lightly floured surface to a 15 x 24 cm (6 x 9½ in) oval.

Divide the cooled lentil mixture among the pizzas, piling it down the centre and leaving a 2.5 cm (1 in) border. Scatter with the feta. Fold the edges up to contain the filling, pinching the ends to create torpedo-shaped pizzas.

Carefully place the pizzas on the trays. Bake for 20 minutes, swapping the trays around halfway through cooking, or until crisp and golden. Serve warm or at room temperature, garnished with the extra coriander.

Eggplant & tomato pizza

If you can't find smoked cheddar, use any other firm smoked cheese.

Preparation time: 20 minutes
Cooking time: 45 minutes
Makes: four 16 x 30 cm (6¼ x 12 in) rectangle pizzas (serves 4)

125 ml (4 fl oz/½ cup) extra virgin olive oil
1 large eggplant (aubergine) (about 500 g/1lb 2 oz),
   cut into 5 mm (¼ in) thick slices
2 red onions, each cut into 8 wedges
1 quantity pizza dough (see page 168)
300 g (10½ oz) fresh buffalo mozzarella cheese,
   thinly sliced

4 small ripe tomatoes, thinly sliced
80 g (2¾ oz) finely grated smoked cheddar cheese
4 garlic cloves, finely chopped
40 g (1½ oz/⅔ cup) fresh breadcrumbs,
   made from day-old bread

Heat 80 ml (2½ fl oz/⅓ cup) of the olive oil in a large frying pan over medium–high heat and cook the eggplant in batches for 2 minutes each side, or until just browned. Drain on paper towel.

Heat the remaining oil in the same pan over medium heat and cook the onion, stirring occasionally, for 10 minutes, or until lightly browned.

Preheat the oven to 230°C (450°F/Gas 8). Place two large, heavy baking trays in the oven to heat.

Cut the dough into four even portions and shape each into a ball. Press each ball to flatten, then use a lightly floured rolling pin to roll out each ball on a piece of non-stick baking paper to a 16 x 30 cm

(6¼ x 12 in) rectangle. Make a border, pressing with your fingertips 2 cm (¾ in) from the edge.

Top the pizzas with the mozzarella cheese, eggplant, tomato and onion. Sprinkle with the smoked cheddar, garlic and breadcrumbs, and season with salt and freshly ground black pepper.

Remove the trays from the oven one at a time to keep them as hot as possible and carefully slide one pizza (still on the baking paper) onto each tray. Bake for 10 minutes, swapping the trays around halfway through cooking, or until the bases are crisp and golden. Bake the remaining two pizzas. Serve immediately.

Tomato & ricotta pizza with olive tapenade

Traditionally, ricotta cheese is made uisng the leftover curds from making parmesan cheese. Today, ricotta cheese is made from skimmed or whole milk, which makes it fattier and creamier than cheese made by the traditional method.

Preparation time: 15 minutes
Cooking time: 10 minutes
Makes: two 25 cm (10 in) round pizzas (serves 4)

1 quantity pizza dough (see page 168)
80 ml (2½ fl oz/⅓ cup) pizza sauce (see page 169)
2 tablespoons olive tapenade (see page 172)

160 g (5¾ oz) firm, fresh ricotta cheese
160 g (5¾ oz) mixed cherry and teardrop tomatoes, halved

Preheat the oven to 220°C (425°F/Gas 7). Place two large, heavy pizza or baking trays in the oven to heat.

Cut the dough into two even portions and shape each into a ball. Press each ball to flatten, then use a lightly floured rolling pin to roll out each ball on a piece of non-stick baking paper to a 25 cm (10 in) round. Make a border, pressing with your fingertips 2 cm (¾ in) from the edge.

Spread the pizzas evenly with the pizza sauce and dollop with the tapenade. Crumble over

the ricotta, arrange the tomato halves on top and season with sea salt and freshly ground black pepper.

Remove the trays from the oven one at a time to keep them as hot as possible and carefully slide one pizza (still on the baking paper) onto each tray. Bake for 10 minutes, swapping the trays around halfway through cooking, or until the bases are golden and cooked through. Serve immediately.

Mixed mushroom & asparagus pizza

The delicately flavoured asparagus shoots need to be cooked with care so as not to damage the fragile tips. Asparagus does not keep for long and ideally should be cooked on the day of purchase.

Preparation time: 10 minutes (+ cooling time)
Cooking time: 45 minutes
Makes: four 25 cm (10 in) square pizzas (serves 4)

8 garlic cloves, peeled
2 tablespoons olive oil
150 g (5½ oz) small button mushrooms
200 g (7 oz) Swiss brown mushrooms, thickly sliced
1 bunch asparagus (about 180 g/6¼ oz)

1 quantity pizza dough (see page 168)
1 quantity roasted tomato pizza sauce (see page 169)
240 g (8¾ oz) fresh buffalo mozzarella cheese, thinly sliced

Preheat the oven to 220°C (425°F/Gas 7). Place two large, heavy baking trays in the oven to heat.

Place the garlic on a double layer of foil, drizzle with 2 teaspoons of the olive oil and seal. Bake for 25 minutes or until soft. Cool slightly and remove from the skins.

Cut half of the button mushrooms in half. Heat a large non-stick frying pan over high heat and add the remaining olive oil. Add all the button and Swiss brown mushrooms, season with salt and freshly ground black pepper and cook for 3–4 minutes, stirring occasionally, or until just tender. Transfer to a plate to cool.

Trim the asparagus and cut each spear into three pieces. Cook the asparagus in salted boiling water for 1 minute, or until par-cooked. Refresh in a bowl of iced water. Drain and set aside.

Cut the dough into four even portions and shape each into a ball. Press each ball to flatten, then use a lightly floured rolling pin to roll out each ball on a piece of non-stick baking paper to a 25 cm (10 in) square.

Spread the pizzas evenly with the pizza sauce, leaving a small border, then top with half the mozzarella cheese, the mushrooms, garlic, asparagus and the remaining mozzarella cheese.

Remove the trays from the oven one at a time to keep them as hot as possible and carefully slide one pizza (still on the baking paper) onto each tray. Bake for 10 minutes, swapping the trays around halfway through cooking. Then bake the remaining two pizzas. Serve immediately.

Pizza con salsa verde

Salsa verde pizza

Bocconcini, meaning 'little bites' in Italian, are egg-sized mozzarella cheeses that originated in Naples and were once made only from the milk of water buffaloes. They are semi-soft, white, rindless, unripened mild cheeses.

Preparation time: 10 minutes
Cooking time: 20 minutes
Makes: four 25 cm (10 in) round pizzas (serves 4)

1 quantity pizza dough (see page 168)
125 ml (4 fl oz/½ cup) extra virgin olive oil
240 g (8¾ oz) bocconcini (fresh baby mozzarella cheese), thinly sliced, drained on paper towel
1 handful finely chopped flat-leaf (Italian) parsley

2 tablespoons salted baby capers, rinsed, drained
4 garlic cloves, chopped
40 g (1½ oz) rocket (arugula), to garnish

Preheat the oven to 230°C (450°F/Gas 8). Place two large, heavy pizza or baking trays in the oven to heat.

Cut the dough into four even portions and shape each into a ball. Press each ball to flatten, then use a lightly floured rolling pin to roll out each ball on a piece of non-stick baking paper to a 25 cm (10 in) round.

Brush the pizzas with half the olive oil, then top with half the bocconcini, leaving a small border.

Sprinkle over the parsley, capers and garlic. Top with the remaining bocconcini.

Remove the trays from the oven one at a time to keep them as hot as possible and carefully slide one pizza (still on the baking paper) onto each tray. Bake for 8–10 minutes, swapping the trays around halfway through cooking, or until the bases are crisp and golden. Bake the remaining two pizzas. Serve the pizzas immediately, topped with the rocket and drizzled with the remaining olive oil.

CALZONE CON BIETOLA E UVETTA

Silverbeet & raisin calzone

Pine nuts add a distinctve flavour to this pizza. Their flavour is enhanced when they are roasted or fried but, because the nuts are very high in oil, they can burn very quickly.

Preparation time: 25 minutes
Cooking time: 45 minutes
Makes: six calzone (serves 6)

1 kg (2 lb 4 oz) silverbeet (Swiss chard)
60 ml (2 fl oz/¼ cup) olive oil, plus extra, for greasing
1 large brown onion, chopped
3 garlic cloves, finely chopped
80 g (2¾ oz/⅓ cup) pine nuts
60 g (2¼ oz/⅓ cup) raisins, roughly chopped

2 tablespoons red wine vinegar
150 g (5½ oz/1½ cups) finely shredded
  parmesan cheese
1½ quantities pizza dough (see page 168)
lemon wedges, to serve

Preheat the oven to 220°C (425°F/Gas 7). Lightly grease two large, heavy baking trays.

Wash the silverbeet leaves and shake dry. Remove the stems and reserve. Finely shred the leaves, then set aside. Trim the ends of the stems and finely chop the stems. Heat the oil in a very large saucepan over medium heat. Add the chopped stems, onion, garlic and pine nuts, and cook, stirring often, for 10 minutes or until the vegetables are soft and the pine nuts are light golden.

Add the silverbeet leaves, raisins and vinegar, increase the heat to high then cook, stirring often, for 5–6 minutes or until the leaves are wilted. Cook for a further 2–3 minutes or until the excess liquid evaporates (the mixture should not be wet). Transfer to a bowl and cool slightly. Stir through the parmesan cheese and season with salt and freshly ground black pepper.

Cut the dough into six even portions and shape each into a ball. Press each ball to flatten, then use a lightly floured rolling pin to roll out each ball on a lightly floured surface to a 23 cm (9 in) round.

Divide the silverbeet mixture among the dough rounds, piling it evenly over one half only and leaving a 1.5 cm (⅝ in) border around the edges. Use a pastry brush or your fingertips to lightly brush the borders with water. Fold the uncovered half of each dough round up and over the filling, then press the edges together to seal well.

Carefully transfer the calzone to the trays, bending them slightly from the middle to make a half-moon shape. Bake for 25 minutes, swapping the trays around halfway through cooking, or until the crusts are golden and cooked through. Serve immediately with lemon wedges.

Mini balsamic onion & goat's cheese pizzas

Goat's cheese is available in a variety of shapes and sizes such as pyramids, cones and cylinders. The flavour can be mild or pronounced, depending on how long the cheese has been aged.

Preparation time: 35 minutes (+ cooling time)
Cooking time: 1 hour 5 minutes
Makes: 46 mini round pizzas

80 ml (2½ fl oz/⅓ cup) olive oil
1.5 kg (3 lb 6 oz) brown onions, halved lengthways, thinly sliced
3 teaspoons caster (superfine) sugar
2 tablespoons balsamic vinegar

1 quantity parmesan cheese pizza dough (see page 168), adding 1 tablespoon dried mint to the flour mixture
300 g (10½ oz) pitted black olives, halved lengthways
220 g (7¾ oz) soft goat's cheese, crumbled
1 handful small mint leaves, to garnish

Heat the olive oil in a very large saucepan over medium heat and cook the onion, stirring often, for 35–40 minutes or until very soft and starting to caramelise. Add the sugar and vinegar and cook, stirring, for 5 minutes or until any excess liquid has evaporated. Season with salt and freshly ground black pepper. Set aside to cool.

Preheat the oven to 230°C (450°F/Gas 8). Line four large, heavy baking trays with non-stick baking paper.

Take a small, walnut-sized portion of dough and roll out on a lightly floured surface to a

6 cm (2½ in) round. Repeat with the remaining dough to make another 45 bases. Place on the trays, leaving 2 cm (¾ in) between each.

Top the pizzas with the onion mixture, olives and goat's cheese.

Bake two trays of pizzas for 10 minutes, swapping the trays around halfway through cooking, or until the bases are crisp and golden. Repeat with the remaining trays of pizzas. Serve the pizzas immediately, garnished with the mint.

Wild mushroom pizza

Store mushrooms in the fridge in a paper bag to allow them to breathe. Don't leave them in plastic as this makes them sweat. Wild mushrooms are best eaten the day they are picked; cultivated mushrooms will last up to three days in the fridge.

Preparation time: 10 minutes
Cooking time: 12 minutes
Makes: one 25 cm (10 in) round pizza (serves 2-4)

100 g (3½ oz) fresh wild mushrooms, such as
   chanterelles or porcini, trimmed but left whole
60 ml (2 fl oz/¼ cup) extra virgin olive oil
½ quantity pizza dough (see page 168)

1 tablespoon chopped thyme
2 small garlic cloves, chopped
extra virgin olive oil, for drizzling

Preheat the oven to 230°C (450°F/Gas 8). Place a large, heavy pizza or baking tray in the oven to heat.

Toss the mushrooms in 1 tablespoon of the oil. Set aside.

Shape the pizza dough into a ball. Flatten the ball, then use a lightly floured rolling pin to roll out on a piece of non-stick baking paper to a 25 cm (10 in) round.

Drizzle the pizza base with oil and scatter with thyme and garlic. Top with the mushrooms and season with salt and freshly ground black pepper,.

Remove the tray from the oven and carefully slide the pizza (still on the baking paper) onto the tray.

Cook for 10–12 minutes or until the base is crisp and the topping cooked. Drizzle with extra virgin olive oil.

Roasted eggplant & garlic pizza

Eggplants (aubergines) are often considered a vegetable, but they are actually a fruit and a member of the same family as the tomato and potato. Buy firm, heavy fruits that have shiny, smooth skins with no brown patches and a distinct cleft in the wider end.

Preparation time: 25 minutes (+ cooling time)
Cooking time: 45 minutes
Makes: four 25 cm (10 in) round pizzas (serves 4)

8 garlic cloves, unpeeled
60 ml (2 fl oz/¼ cup) olive oil
1 eggplant (aubergine) (about 450 g/1 lb)
1 quantity wholemeal pizza dough (see page 168)
1 quantity pizza sauce (see page 169)

200 g (7 oz) fresh buffalo mozzarella cheese, thinly sliced
1 small handful oregano leaves
105 g (3½ oz/½ cup) mint & chilli pesto (see page 173)
1 small handful flat-leaf (Italian) parsley leaves

Preheat the oven to 200°C (400°F/Gas 6). Line a baking tray with non-stick baking paper.

Place the garlic on a double layer of foil, drizzle with 2 teaspoons of the olive oil and seal. Cut the eggplant into 2 cm (¾ in) chunks and place in a bowl with the remaining olive oil. Season with salt and toss to combine. Spread the eggplant on the lined tray. Place the garlic parcel on the tray with the eggplant. Roast for 25 minutes, or until the eggplant is just tender and starting to colour. Set aside to cool. Remove the garlic from the skins.

Increase the oven to 220°C (425°F/Gas 7). Place two large, heavy pizza or baking trays in the oven to heat.

Cut the dough into four even portions and shape each into a ball. Press each ball to flatten, then use a lightly floured rolling pin to roll out each ball on a piece of non-stick baking paper to a 25 cm (10 in) round.

Spread the pizzas evenly with the pizza sauce, then top with half the mozzarella cheese, the eggplant, garlic, oregano and the remaining mozzarella cheese.

Remove the trays from the oven one at a time to keep them as hot as possible and carefully slide one pizza (still on the baking paper) onto each tray. Bake for 10 minutes, swapping the trays around halfway through cooking, or until the bases are crisp and golden. Bake the remaining two pizzas. Serve the pizzas immediately, topped with the mint and chilli pesto, and sprinkled with the parsley.

Pizza con patate e arucola
Potato & rocket pizza

Taleggio cheese is a semi-hard cheese, like a slightly firmer mozzarella cheese, or a brie. It has a thin crust and a strong aroma, but a comparatively mild flavour. You can substitute brie for the taleggio cheese but your pizza won't have the same distinctive taste.

Preparation time: 10 minutes
Cooking time: 12 minutes
Makes: one 30 cm (12 in) round pizzas (serves 4–6)

½ quantity pizza dough (see page 168)
2 tablespoons extra virgin olive oil
1 potato, very thinly sliced

100 g (3½ oz) taleggio cheese, cut into small pieces
1 handful rocket (arugula)
extra virgin olive oil, for drizzling

Preheat the oven to 230°C (450°F/Gas 8). Place a large, heavy pizza or baking tray in the oven to heat.

Shape the pizza dough into a ball. Flatten the ball, then use a lightly floured rolling pin to roll out on a piece of non-stick baking paper to a 25 cm (10 in) round.

Drizzle the pizza base with oil. Cover with a layer of potato, leaving a thin border, sprinkle with the taleggio cheese and season.

Remove the tray from the oven and carefully slide the pizza (still on the baking paper) onto the tray.

Cook for 8–12 minutes, or until the potato is cooked. Garnish with the rocket, drizzle with oil and scatter with rocket.

Use a lightly floured rolling pin to roll out the pizza dough on a piece of non-stick paper.

Manosha (Arabic pizza)

Feta cheese has a tangy, salty flavour and can range from soft to semi-hard. Most feta cheese you find in supermarkets is sold in chunks or blocks in brine, in packs or tubs. Today feta cheese is made in many countries but it originated in Greece.

Preparation time: 15 minutes
Cooking time: 15 minutes
Makes: eight 13 cm (5 in) round pizzas (serves 8 as a snack or starter)

2 tablespoons olive oil, plus extra, for greasing
1 quantity pizza dough (see page 168)
250 g (9 oz) feta cheese, coarsely crumbled

1 teaspoon cumin seeds
1½ teaspoons dried dill or mint
lemon cheeks, to serve

Preheat the oven to 220°C (425°F/Gas 7). Lightly grease two large, heavy pizza or baking trays with olive oil.

Cut the dough into eight even portions and shape each into a ball. Press each ball to flatten, then use a lightly floured rolling pin to roll out each ball on a lightly floured surface to a 13 cm (5 in) round. Place the pizzas on the trays, spacing evenly. Top

with the feta cheese, cumin and dill or mint then drizzle with the olive oil.

Bake the pizzas for 15 minutes, swapping the trays around halfway through cooking, or until the bases are crisp and golden. Serve immediately or at room temperature, accompanied by the lemon cheeks.

Chapter 6

DESSERT

Pizzas can make a delicious and easy dessert! Top your normal base with
seasonal fruit; drizzle with chocolate or caramel and serve with a scoop
of ice cream or a spoonful of thick cream.

Blueberry-banana dessert pizza

When buying blueberries, choose firm, plump berries without any squashed or leaking fruit—these will be stale and tasteless. You can substitute strawberries for the blueberries if you like.

Preparation time: 10 minutes
Cooking time: 30 minutes
Makes: one 28 cm (11¼ in) pizza (serves 6)

220 g (7¾ oz/1½ cups) plain (all-purpose) flour
30 g (1 oz) butter
120 ml (4 fl oz/½ cup) milk
120 g (4¼ oz/½ cup) mascarpone cheese
2 teaspoons demerara sugar

2 small bananas, sliced
200 g (7 oz) blueberries
60 g (2¼ oz/½ cup) chopped pecans
2 teaspoons demerara sugar, extra
2 teaspoons melted butter for brushing

Preheat the oven to 210°C (415°F/ Gas 6–7). Brush a 30 cm (12 in) pizza tray with melted butter.

Place the flour and butter in a food processor bowl and process for 20 seconds, or until the mixture resembles fine breadcrumbs. Add the milk and process for a further 30 seconds until the mixture comes together.

Turn out onto a lightly floured surface and knead gently for 1 minute, or until smooth. Roll out to 28 cm (11¼ in). Place onto the prepared tray and fold the edges inward to form a rim.

Spread the mascarpone over the base, then sprinkle with sugar. Arrange the sliced banana in a ring along the edge of the pizza and in a smaller ring towards the centre.

Fill the inside of the rings with blueberries. Sprinkle with pecans and extra sugar. Brush the pastry rim with a little melted butter.

Bake for 25 minutes, or until the pastry crust is golden. Serve warm with cream or ice cream, if desired.

Knead the dough by stretching it away from you and then folding it back on itself.

Apple & ginger dessert pizza

Preparation time: 10 minutes
Cooking time: 30 minutes
Makes: two 25 cm (10 in) pizzas (serves 6)

125 g (4½ oz/1 cup) sultanas (golden raisins)
80 ml (2½ fl oz/⅓ cup) brandy
60 g (2¼ oz) butter
3 teaspoons ground ginger
80 ml (2½ fl oz/⅓ cup) maple syrup

1 quantity pizza dough (see page 168)
2 red apples, cored and cut into wedges
2 green apples, cored and cut into wedges
1 tablespoon melted butter
thick cream, to serve

Preheat the oven to 220°C (425°F/Gas 7). Place two large, heavy baking trays in the oven to heat.

Combine the sultanas and brandy in small bowl and set aside.

Melt the butter in a pan, then add the ginger and stir to combine. Add 80 ml (2½ fl oz/⅓ cup) water and the maple syrup, then cook over low heat for 4 minutes, or until thickened slightly. Cool.

Cut the dough into two even portions and shape each into a ball. Press each ball to flatten, then use a lightly floured rolling pin to roll out each ball on a piece of non-stick baking paper to a 25 cm (10 in) square.

Drain the sultanas and sprinkle over the base. Arrange the apple slices on top and drizzle with syrup. Brush the edge of the pizza base with a little melted butter. Bake for 25 minutes, or until the crust is golden brown. Serve warm with thick cream.

BASICS

An important step in mastering any cuisine is learning the basic recipes and techniques. Here are the ones that no pizza cook should be without.

Pizza dough

Preparation time: 20 minutes (+ 1 hour proving time)
Makes: enough for four 25 cm (10 in) thin-based pizzas or two 25 cm (10 in) thick-based pizzas

400 g (14 oz/2⅔ cups) plain (all-purpose) flour
14 g (½ oz/1 tablespoon) dried yeast
2 teaspoons sugar

1 teaspoon salt
250 ml (9 fl oz/1 cup) lukewarm water
3 teaspoons olive oil

Place the flour, yeast, sugar and salt in a bowl and make a well in the centre. Combine the water and olive oil and add to the flour mixture. Use a wooden spoon and then your hands to mix to a dough.

Turn onto a lightly floured surface and knead for 5 minutes, or until smooth and elastic.

Place the dough in an oiled bowl and turn to coat lightly in the oil. Cover loosely with a clean, slightly damp tea towel (dish towel) or plastic wrap and set aside in a warm, draught-free place for 1 hour or until doubled in size.

Knock back the dough by punching your fist into the centre of the dough. Turn onto a lightly floured surface and knead for 2–3 minutes, or until smooth and elastic. Use immediately as directed.

VARIATIONS
Wholemeal pizza dough: Replace the plain flour with 400 g (14 oz/2⅔ cups) wholemeal (whole-wheat) flour and add an extra 50 ml (1½ fl oz) lukewarm water.

Gluten-free pizza dough: Replace the plain flour with 400 g (14 oz/2⅔ cups) gluten-free flour and add 1 extra tablespoon of lukewarm water.

Rosemary pizza dough: After kneading in step 2, add 2 teaspoons very finely chopped rosemary and knead for another 1 minute to incorporate.

Parmesan cheese pizza dough: After kneading in step 2, add 40 g (1½ oz) finely grated parmesan cheese and knead for another 1 minute to incorporate.

Far left: Knock back the dough by punching your fist into the centre of the dough.
Left: Divide the dough into the required number of portions.

Pizza sauce

Although you can make this sauce using fresh tomatoes, it would take a lot of time to prepare and cook them. Good tinned tomatoes are picked at the peak of freshness and are often better than fresh tomatoes, which are picked early and ripened artificially.

Preparation time: 10 minutes
Cooking time: 25 minutes
Makes: 250 ml (9 fl oz/1 cup)

1 tablespoon olive oil
¼ brown onion, finely chopped
1 garlic clove, finely chopped

400 g (14 oz) tinned whole tomatoes
5 basil leaves
pinch of sugar, or to taste

Heat the oil in a small saucepan over low heat. Add the onion and garlic and cook, stirring occasionally, for 6 minutes or until softened.

Add the tomatoes and basil, then use a potato masher to crush the tomatoes. Simmer, stirring occasionally, for 15–18 minutes or until sauce thickens. Taste and season with sugar, salt and freshly ground black pepper. Set aside to cool to room temperature.

VARIATIONS
Roasted tomato pizza sauce: Halve 700 g (1 lb 9 oz) roma (plum) tomatoes. Place on a baking tray, cut sides up, drizzle with 1 tablespoon olive oil and sprinkle with the leaves from 4 thyme sprigs. Roast at 180°C (350°F/Gas 4) for 30–40 minutes, or until lightly roasted. Follow recipe for pizza sauce, using the roasted tomatoes instead of tinned tomatoes.

Tomato & chilli pizza sauce: Add 1 finely chopped small red chilli with the onion and garlic.

Herb pizza sauce: Stir 1 tablespoon finely snipped chives and 1 tablespoon finely chopped flat-leaf (Italian) parsley through the sauce at the end of cooking.

Stir in the tomato and herbs to make a thick sauce.

Bread dough

Preparation time: 20 minutes (+ 1-1½ hours proving time)
Makes: one loaf

2 teaspoons dried yeast or 15 g (½ oz) fresh yeast
250 g (9 oz/2 cups) strong plain (all-purpose) flour

3 tablespoons olive oil
½ teaspoon salt

Mix the yeast with 125 ml (4 fl oz/½ cup) warm water. Leave for 10 minutes in a warm place until the yeast becomes frothy. If it does not bubble and foam in this time, throw it away and start again.

Sift the flour into a large bowl. Add the olive oil, salt and the yeast mixture. Mix until the dough clumps together and forms a ball.

Turn out onto a lightly floured surface. Knead the dough, adding a little more flour or a few drops of warm water if necessary, until you have a soft dough that is not sticky but is dry to the touch. Knead for 10 minutes, or until smooth and the impression made by a finger springs back immediately.

Rub the inside of a large bowl with olive oil. Roll the ball of dough around in the bowl to coat with oil, then cut a shallow cross on the top of the ball with a sharp knife. Leave the dough in the bowl, cover with a tea towel or put in a plastic bag and leave in a draught-free spot for 1–1½ hours, or until the dough has doubled in size (or leave in the fridge for 8 hours to rise slowly).

Knock back the dough by punching it with your fist several times to expel the air and then knead it again for a couple of minutes. (At this stage, the dough can be stored in the fridge for 4 hours, or frozen. Bring back to room temperature before continuing.) Leave in a warm place to rise until doubled in size.

Far left: Use flour that is packaged as 'strong' or 'bread' flour. You can use plain (all-purpose) flour or a mixture of plain and wholemeal, but the results won't be as good.

Left: Knock down the bread dough by punching it with your fist several times.

Pasta focaccia

Focaccia dough

Make the dough in a large bowl so you have enough room to bring it together. Knead on a well-floured surface until the dough is really elastic. Use the heel of your hand to stretch it into a rectangle.

Preparation time: 20 minutes (+ 3-3½ hours proving time)
Makes: two 38 x 28 cm (15 x 11¼ inch) rectangle focaccia

½ teaspoon caster (superfine) sugar
2 teaspoons dried yeast or 15 g (½ oz) fresh yeast
810 ml (28 fl oz) lukewarm water
1 kg (2 lb 4 oz) plain (all-purpose) flour

2 teaspoons salt
2 tablespoons olive oil
cornmeal

Put the sugar and yeast in a small bowl and stir in 60 ml (2 fl oz/¼ cup)of the water. Leave in a draught-free spot to activate. If the yeast does not bubble and foam in 5 minutes, discard it and start again.

Mix the flour and salt in a bowl or in a food processor fitted with a plastic blade. Add the olive oil, the yeast mixture and three-quarters of the remaining water. Mix, then add the rest of the water, a little at a time, until the dough loosely clumps together. Transfer to a lightly floured surface and knead for 8 minutes until smooth, or until the impression made by a finger springs back immediately.

Rub the inside of a large bowl with olive oil. Roll the ball of dough around in the bowl to coat it with oil, then cut a shallow cross on the top of the ball with a sharp knife. Leave the dough in the bowl, cover with a tea towel or put in a plastic bag and leave in a draught-free spot for 1–1½ hours until doubled in size (or leave in the fridge for 8 hours to rise slowly).

Punch down the dough to its original size, then divide into two portions. (At this stage, the dough can be stored in the fridge for 4 hours, or frozen. Bring back to room temperature before continuing.) Roll each portion of dough out to a 28 x 20 cm (11¼ x 8 in) rectangle, then use the heels of your hands, working from the centre of the dough outwards, to make a 38 x 28 cm (15 x 11¼ in) rectangle.

Lightly oil 2 baking trays and dust with cornmeal. Put a portion of dough in the centre of each tray and press out to fill the tray. Slide the trays inside a plastic bag. Seal and leave in a draught-free spot for 2 hours to rise again. The focaccia dough is now ready to use, as instructed in the recipe.

Olive tapenade

Traditionally, a tapaenade is a paste of black or green olives, anchovies and capers, pounded in a mortar and pestle, and seasoned with olive oil and lemon juice. The name comes from *tapeno*, an Italian word for 'capers'. Also sold ready-made in jars.

Preparation time: 10 minutes
Makes: 250 g (9 oz/1 cup)

205 g (7¼ oz/1⅓ cups) pitted kalamata olives
1 garlic clove, chopped
1 tablespoon salted baby capers, rinsed, drained
6 anchovy fillets, drained, chopped

15 g (½ oz) flat-leaf (Italian) parsley leaves
finely grated zest of ½ lemon
1 tablespoon lemon juice
80 ml (2½ fl oz/⅓ cup) extra virgin olive oil

Place the olives, garlic, capers, anchovies and parsley in a small food processor and pulse until roughly chopped.

Stir through the lemon zest and juice and the olive oil. Season with salt and freshly ground black pepper.

VARIATIONS
Green olive tapenade: Replace the kalamata olives with green olives. (Pitted unstuffed green olives are often hard to find so use a small knife to remove the flesh from 300 g (10½ oz) whole large green olives—you should have 200 g/7 oz flesh.)

Semi-dried tomato tapenade: Replace the kalamata olives with 200 g (7 oz) semi-dried (sun-blushed) tomatoes. Replace the parsley with the same amount of basil leaves.

PESTO

Pesto

Preparation time: 10 minutes
Makes: 210 g (7½ oz/1 cup)

55 g (2 oz) basil leaves
1 garlic clove, finely chopped
50 g (1¾ oz/⅓ cup) finely grated parmesan cheese

40 g (1½ oz/¼ cup) pine nuts
125 ml (4 fl oz/½ cup) olive oil

Place the basil, garlic, parmesan cheese and pine nuts in a food processor and pulse until roughly chopped.

With the motor running, gradually add the oil to combine. Season with salt and freshly ground black pepper.

VARIATIONS
Rocket pesto: Replace the basil with 55 g (2 oz/1⅔ cups) wild rocket (arugula).

Mint & chilli pesto: Replace the basil with 20 g (¾ oz) mint leaves and 10 g (¼ oz) flat-leaf (Italian) parsley leaves. Add ½ long red chilli, seeded and chopped.

Tips for a better pizza

To reduce the proving time by about half, divide the pizza dough into portions (according to the number of pizzas you are going to make) before setting aside to prove.

When cutting the pizza dough into portions, use a floured knife to make it easy and stick-free.

Use good-quality, heavy pizza or baking trays to cook the pizzas—they will retain heat more effectively and help give you a crisp base.

If possible, always preheat the pizza or baking trays in the oven so that the pizzas can go straight onto hot trays. Hot, good-quality trays will result in

crisp bases—just be careful when transferring the pizzas onto them before baking.

Roll out the pizzas on non-stick baking paper then use this to lift the pizzas onto the hot trays to avoid burning your fingers.

You can use pizza stones to cook all the pizzas in this book to help achieve crisp bases. However, remember that your pizzas will take less time to cook—usually 2–5 minutes less.

Swapping the trays around about halfway through cooking will ensure that your pizzas cook evenly and will be ready at the same time.

INDEX

Published in 2018 by Murdoch Books, an imprint of Allen & Unwin

Murdoch Books Australia
83 Alexander Street
Crows Nest NSW 2065
Phone: +61 (0) 2 8425 0100
Fax: +61 (0) 2 9906 2218
murdochbooks.com.au
info@murdochbooks.com.au

Murdoch Books UK
Ormond House
26–27 Boswell Street
London WC1N 3JZ
Phone: +44 (0) 20 8785 5995
murdochbooks.co.uk
info@murdochbooks.co.uk

For Corporate Orders & Custom Publishing, contact our Business Development Team at
salesenquiries@murdochbooks.com.au.

Publisher: Corinne Roberts
Project Editor: Ice Cold Publishing
Photographer: Michele Aboud
Stylist: Sarah de Nardi
Food Editor: Katy Holder
Recipe Development: Chrissy Freer, Sonia Greig, Leanne Kitchen and Kathy Snowball
Production Manager: Lou Adler

A cataloguing-in-publication entry is available from the catalogue of the
National Library of Australia at nla.gov.au.

9781760631895 ANZ
9781760634360 UK

A catalogue record for this book is available from the British Library.

Printed and bound by Leo Paper Group, China

IMPORTANT: Those who might be at risk from the effects of salmonella poisoning (the elderly, pregnant
women, young children and those suffering from immune deficiency diseases) should consult their doctor with
any concerns about eating raw eggs.

OVEN GUIDE: You may find cooking times vary depending on the oven you are using. For fan-forced ovens,
as a general rule, set the oven temperature to 20°C (70°F) lower than indicated in the recipe.

MEASURES GUIDE: We have used 20 ml (4 teaspoon) tablespoon measures. If you are using a
15 ml (3 teaspoon) tablespoon add an extra teaspoon of the ingredient for each tablespoon specified.